HOMBU

Indian life in the Brazilian jungle

HARALD SCHULTZ

HOMBU

THE MACMILLAN COMPANY - NEW YORK - 1962

Printed in the Netherlands

Library of Congress catalog card number: 62 - 19993

HOMBU

The rapid economic development of South America, especially Brazil, has had its influence on the primitive inhabitants, such as the Suyá tribe in Central Brazil and the Caiapó in the wide plains of the middle Xingu River. These people, until recently unapproachable because of their unfriendly attitude, have been affected by the changes in their tribal regions, and have emerged and entered into friendly relations with the whites.

Other Indian tribes, whose names have not until now been known, are being discovered in the far corners of the primeval forests. The day is not distant when the last blank places in the immense, unexplored primeval forests of the Amazon will be filled in on the map.

At the behest of the Brazilian Government the author journeyed every year for two decades to little-known, as well as little visited Indians, some without any previous contact with the outside world. In addition to his scientific exploration of Indian life, he set out from the beginning to use his camera to capture a lifelike picture of his primitive friends.

He spent many months with certain Indian tribes. All the photographs in this book are genuine proof of real Indian life. None is staged.

HOMBU in the Crahó Indian language means 'Look here!' With this illustrated volume the author will attempt to bring to the reader that which is human in the Indian, that incomprehensible comprehensible that unites all mankind all over the world because it is present in all of us. Hombu!

Harald Schultz May, 1962

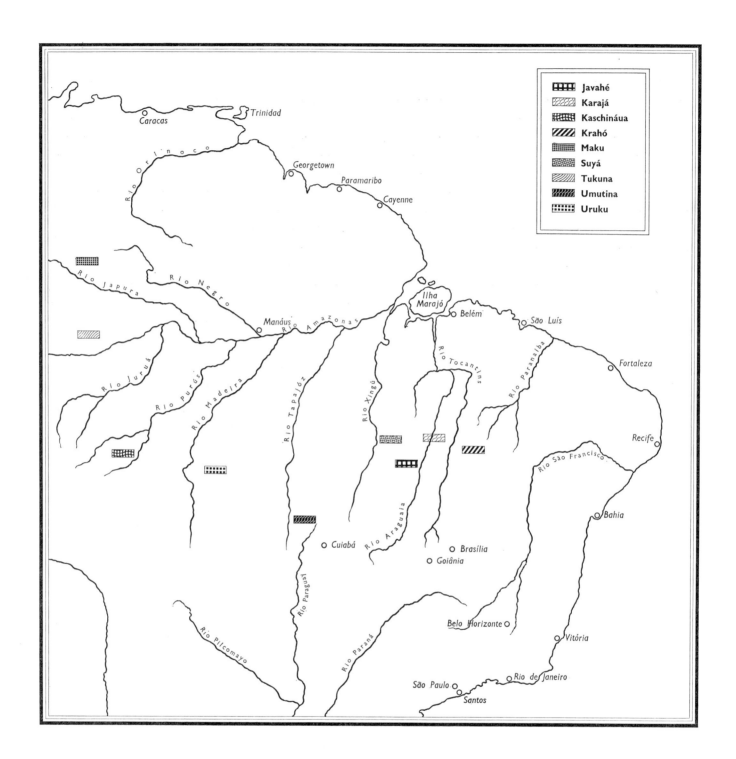

Legend:
- Javahé
- Karajá
- Kaschináua
- Krahó
- Maku
- Suyá
- Tukuna
- Umutina
- Uruku

CRAHÓ

Some five hundred Crahó Indians live in four villages in the wide savanna east of the Tocantins River, in the Brazilian central states of Goiás and Maranhão. Their villages are built in a winding circular manner. A broad clean road connects the houses located on the outside. The village square can be reached from every house by a straight path. This square, which is located in the middle of the village, serves as the assembly point and center of its social and political activity. The head of the government of a Crahó village is a chief who is elected by the 'Council of Elders.' There are two so-called administrative divisions with junior chiefs, and four officials for each division. One of these divisions is active in the winter during the rainy season, the other in the summer during the dry season.

The members of the tribe are divided into two parts – one is supposed to have descended from the sun and the other from the moon. Many myths and legends tell of the adventures and experiences of the early ancestors of the Crahó Indians. In addition to these divisions, boys and men are classified in accordance with their membership in sports and ceremonial groups. Singing and games are favored daily occupations. The conductors of male and female choruses are at the same time the composers and authors of the many songs. Hunting and agricultural pursuits provide the meager daily nourishment.

The language of the Crahó Indians belongs to the great Brazilian family of languages of the Gê peoples.

The appropriate pictures are to be found on the cover, the frontispiece, 1, 2, 6, 7, 9, 11, 14, 18, 20, 23, 24, 26, 28 (color), 33, 34, 35, 36, 37, 46, 48, 49, 50, 51, 52, 53, 56 (color), 57, 58, 82, 83, 84, 98 (color), 99, 100, 103, 104 (color), 105

JAVAHÉ and CARAJÁ

About eight hundred Javahé and Carajá Indians live on the riversides and sandbanks of the Araguaya river, which flows through Central Brazil and empties into the Tocantins. The mode of life of both tribes is, with some insignificant differences, the same. The most important source of nourishment of the Javahés is agriculture, while the Carajás are primarily fishermen. Both tribes are skilled in the making of gaily colored clay figurines, pottery, splendidly decorated weapons, colored feather ornaments, as well as in weaving and carving.

Fertility dances with multicolored masks and fancy dress are put on during the hot and dry summers on the many sandbanks. In the cooler rainy season there are also dances for the initiation of the youth and the veneration of ancestors. These dances are the visible expressions of religious ideas.

Their language stands alone and it is not possible to associate it with any other known Indian language family of Brazil. The Javahés and Carajás are in constant touch with their Brazilian neighbors: traders, peasants, fishermen, sheep raisers, upon whom they are partly dependent economically. The Brazilian Federal Government has made Bananal Island, which is formed by the two arms of the Araguaya River, a national park, and is attempting to attract tourists to this beautiful region.

The appropriate pictures are 4, 5, 15, 29, 30, 31, 32, 38, 45, 65, 69, 70, 71, 74, 85, 88, 95, 96, 102, 119, 120, 121, 122, 123, 124, 125, 126.

MAKÚ-GUARIBA

Various little-known Indian tribes who live in the dense primeval forests between the Rio Negro and the Japura in the State of Amazonas are known by the collective name of Makú.

An independent and partially savage tribe is the Makú-Guariba, whom the author visited in 1958. Until about ten years ago these Indians avoided any relations with Brazilian settlers. In the past there have been reports of bloody feuds between the Makús and the rubber gatherers and other invaders of their forests.

The Makú-Guariba are agriculturists and hunters. Fishing is of slight economic importance. At certain seasons when the forest streams are well stocked the natives fish with the aid of a poisonous substance which is grown in their fields and is used to irritate the mucus membrane of the fish. The fish caught in this manner are edible.

In hunting they employ blowguns exclusively, using small arrows, the points of which are poisoned with curare. This very potent poison is prepared by a young Indian who is initiated into the secrets of its making and who carries out his task in a concealed place in the forest. During the several days of the preparation of the poison, the Indian must abstain from any kind of nourishment.

During the harvest of the pupunha-palm fruit which plays an important role in the food supply, the men blow on short, thick reeds. These resemble the Jurupari reeds of the Rio Negro tribes, and the player must not be seen by the women, otherwise the Makú believe that great misfortune will befall the tribe.

The manual skills of the Makú-Guariba are very meager. Outside of plaited flat receptacles made of straw and portable hampers, they possess earthenware pots, wooden mortars, hammocks made of bast or cotton, and smaller objects of daily life, such as wooden spoons and bast beaters.

The exact number of Makú-Guariba in their remote villages could not be ascertained.

The appropriate illustrations are 8 (color), 17 (color), 43, 44, 80.

UMUTINA

Several hundred Umutinas lived until 1911, in a few villages of the riparian forests of the upper Paraguay streams in the north of the Brazilian state of Mato Grosso. These Indians furiously defended their native soil against the foreign invaders, who were searching in their forests for the precious medicinal plant, ipecacuanha, and in their rivers for gold and diamonds. When peace returned to the land, epidemics broke out, in which hundreds of the natives perished. The few who survived found a refuge in the Indian Reservation 'Fraternidade Indigena' (Indian Brotherhood).

During the years 1943 and 1945 the author visited the remnant of the independent Umutinas and stayed eight months with them. Their main source of food was the cultivation of many useful plants on wide fields, which were annually cleared, burned over, and newly planted. A second source of food was fishing with bow and arrow or tibmó poison. Game was becoming scarce and timid in their forests. Women gathered edible roots, mushrooms, fruit, and wild honey.

The village community was composed of households whose female members were blood relatives. The people lived in rectangular stone houses. The oldest female member was the most respected person in matters concerning tribal lore. An energetic mature male served as the counselor in domestic matters. In time of war a leader was appointed, but in time of peace he had no influence.

The Umutinas venerate Haipuku as the creator of the first human beings, who, according to them were born from the calf of his leg. There are also mentioned in their origin myths various medicine men who were instrumental in bringing into the world nourishing plants, and placing fish in the streams.

The sun and the moon are two men who are friends and have had many adventures. In these experiences the sun was successful, while the foolish moon perished and had to be brought to life anew by the sun. If, during the course of the year, a death occurs, just before the maize harvest the Umutinas perform the magnificent ceremonial of the dead. In eighteen different solemn performances, masked dancers represent the souls of dead relatives. The straw of the masks and fancy dress is used to plait mats, with which the Umutinas associate the ideas of resurrection as set forth in their myths. The language of the Umutinas is related to that of the Boróro language group, but culturally they have nothing in common with those tribes.

The appropriate illustrations are 10, 19, 25, 27, 59, 60, 64, 68, 127.

CASHINÁUA

In his expedition in 1951, the author found that some eight hundred Cashináua Indians still lived in the forests of Curanja in the head waters of the Purus, which is one of the great southern Amazonas rivers. Only recently have they established friendly relations with the Brazilians and Peruvians living in the border regions of the two countries. Since that time the Cashináuas have settled near the white population whose tools they value. Fearful epidemics have, however, reduced the tribe within a few years to some ninety or a hundred persons. A second Cashináua group lives scattered in the primeval forests of Tarauacá in the river region of the upper Juruá River in Amazonas.

Their various objects of daily use testify to their high sense of beauty. The artistic craftsmanship of these dwellers of the primeval forest is to be seen in the gorgeous and varicolored woven work, the splendid feather ornaments, the richly decorated weapons, the very beautiful plaited objects, the highly developed art of ceramics and ornaments made from cotton with animal teeth and mother-of-pearl woven in. For some years American anthropologists and language experts have lived among the Cashináuas in order to study their language and culture. The language of the Cashináuas belongs to the Pano group.

The appropriate illustrations are 12, 13, 16, 21, 22, 39, 40, 41, 42, 54, 61, 76, 77, 78, 79, 87, 89, 90, 92, 97, 101, 106, 107.

SUYÁ

At the end of 1959 the hitherto unfriendly Suyá Indians appeared in their bark canoes at the mouth of the Suyá-Missu River at the source region of the upper Xingu, one of the great tributaries of the lower Amazon. They came to establish amicable relations with the settlement of the well-known Villas-Boas brothers, Diauarum, which for two decades has taken care of the many Indian tribes who took up residence there.
Around sixty Suyás live in three communal houses in their village not far from the mouth of their river. The details of their mode of life are little known. The earliest information about the Suyás comes from the famous German explorer, Karl von den Steinen. In 1884 he traveled over the Xingu region and, although they were not entirely friendly, for several days, he was in touch with the (at that time) populous Suyá tribe.
The author spent the months of September and October, 1960, as the first white visitor in a long time at their forest camp. His observations will be published in a leading technical journal.
The tribe consists of two groups with a chief for each. While in general monogamy is practiced, the chiefs have two or three wives. Married men carry a disc of light wood on their perforated lower lip.
They depend for food on fishing, hunting, agriculture, and the collection of fruit and wild honey.

The language of the Suyás belongs to the great family of Gê peoples.

Appropriate illustrations are 3, 35, 47, 81.

URUKÚ

The Urukús live in the dense primeval forests of the upper Gy-Parana, a tributary of the Madeira which flows into the Amazon.
Until about ten years ago these Indians fought with weapons against the rubber gatherers in their region. Today they are peaceful and to a certain extent work with the civilized inhabitants.
The joint families are linked on paternal lines and are presided over by the founders. The families live in roomy straw houses whose walls reach the ground. The founder of the family has from two to three wives, while as far as the junior members are concerned monogamy seems to predominate, until a new independent family is founded.
The entire Urukú tribe consists of from two to three hundred souls. The number is difficult to ascertain, since most of them live in scattered 'malócas' in the forests or in joint family households which have never been visited.
The main sources of food come from agriculture and hunting. The artisan abilities of these Indians are meager. They are limited to the preparation of simple bows and arrows, some plaiting, and some primitive pottery making. Feather adornment is seldom seen and is not particularly artistic. The only musical instrument is a small bamboo flute. The Urukús have for their neighbors the Digüt. Both tribes are closely associated and their intercourse is facilitated by similarity of language. In early times the Urukús had the reputation of kidnapping the women of their neighbors. The Suruims, a neighboring tribe, are feared by both the Urukú and the Digüt. The Suruims are supposed to have emigrated to the upper course of their tribal river, but the fear of them has remained.
The language of the Urukús and Digüt belongs to the Rama-Rama group which blends in the great Tupi language family.

The appropriate illustrations are 55, 75, 91.

5

TUCUNA

On the border region of Brazil, Peru, and Colombia, on the upper Amazon, live about five to six thousand Tucuna Indians. They live in large houses erected on piles on the banks of the many lakes and tributaries of the main stream. Each of these houses is occupied by one or several families, who are related through the male line. Most of the Tucunas are employed by the Brazilian, Peruvian, and Colombian settlers as rubber gatherers, hunters, fishermen, and laborers. Despite this close association with civilization, the Tucunas have retained many of their tribal traditions. Initiation ceremonies usher in the particular life periods of girls and boys.

The most important festivity in the life of a woman is her initiation into maidenhood. Upon reaching a certain age boys also go through a similar ritual.

The Tucunas show their artistic ability by producing colorful costumes, a variety of expressive masks, beautiful pottery, decorated mats, highly polished puppets made of hardwood, and beautiful necklaces made from the hardest tucum palm nut shells, carved to represent all kinds of animals. Excellent boats and light manageable paddles are favorite trade articles. A Brazilian explorer of German descent, Curt Nimuendaju, who was thought by this tribe to be a risen divinity, wrote an important treatise on this interesting Indian tribe. The title of the work is *The Tucuna* (University of California Press, Berkeley and Los Angeles, U.S.A.).

The appropriate illustrations are 62 (color), 63 (color), 66 (color), 67 (color), 72 (color), 86 (color), 93 (color), 108, 109, 110, 111, 112, 113, 114, 115, 116, 117 (color), 118 (color), 128, and the back of the book jacket.

MARAJÓ ISLAND

Archeological Discovery Sites

The Island of Marajó is located in the estuary delta of the Amazon, and covers an area approximately the size of Belgium.

Before the discovery of Brazil this island was inhabited at various times by different Indian tribes. Some of these tribes have produced pottery of high artistic value, which to this day is to be found in the so-called 'mounds' on which are built dwelling places and cemeteries. These 'mounds' were artificially built for the purpose of the protection of the inhabitants of Marajó Island from the annual floods which put most parts of the island under water.

Today no Indian tribes live on Marajó Island. Large Brazilian landowners use the lush pastures for profitable cattle raising. Yet the 'Ilha do Marajó' remains for archeologists an interesting and rewarding excavation site.

The appropriate illustration is 94.

THE DESCRIPTION
OF THE ILLUSTRATIONS

Frontispiece

Next to games, singing and dancing are the favorite diversions of the Crahó Indians. Every morning before sunrise and every evening after sundown the youths assemble on the village square. Girls and women line up in a long row. They sing and wave their arms, rhythmically accompanying the singing. The young men dance in front of them, following the beat of the gourd rattle of the song leader who, while singing and dancing, conducts the choral chant.

In every village there are to be found one or several 'best female singers,' who usually have pleasant, loud and deep alto voices. Their duty is, as soon as they hear the sound of the leader's rattle, to stop whatever they are doing – working or resting – and appear on the square ready to sing. The beautiful sound of their voices is to induce the other women and girls to collect on the square for singing. The best female singer wears an honor decoration, a woven cotton scarf dyed red, bestowed upon her by the young men of the village. Later she will use this scarf as a strap to carry her child. The tufts are made of cotton threads on which are arranged seeds of a certain kind of grass. The red dye of the scarf is derived from the oleaginous pulp of the urucu shrub which is planted by many Indians. From time to time the scarf's red color must be renewed by rubbing it with this dye substance.

1 *Cratchet is a Crahó Indian*

He calls me itó, which means 'my brother.' When I am in his village he is my shadow. 'You whites are not tactful,' he complains. When he, his young wife, and two-year-old son visited us in the great city of São Paolo, his long hair and his elongated perforated earlobes (in which he wears white wooden discs when he is in his home village) attracted considerable attention. Often people asked him, 'To what tribe do you belong?' 'Where do you come from?' and pointing to his long hair, asked him whether he was a man or woman. This continuously repeated curiosity irritated Cratchet. 'When a white man comes to visit our village, we do not annoy him the way you do. We speak quietly and at a distance about him, but nobody is so impertinent as you are.'

The wooden ear disc is a sign of the Crahós male dignity. When the Crahó becomes old, and that means thirty-five to forty years, he removes the ear discs.

Cratchet's head clearly illustrates the accepted hair fashion for both sexes, the object of which is to create a twosided crown of hair on either side of the head. At first the hair below the crown is cut so closely that the scalp, like a bright line, becomes visible. When the hair has grown in again, the wife renews the typical haircut.

Many Indian youths have soft and smooth faces, consequently they frequently appear somewhat feminine in photographs. However, they are strong fellows, hardened by exercise, very muscular, and make good field workers.

Cratchet is one of the most persistent and successful hunters of his village. As a youth he was the most feared Don Juan! The color of the Indians' eyes is deep brown. Their eyes can be so dark that the black pupils can be seen only in a strong light. The Indians vary as to character, just as we do. Keen observers of human beings can learn much from the carriage, behavior, and facial expression of a fellow human being. As far as Cratchet's face was concerned, the same presuppositions apply, though the racial strangeness may confuse some observers.

2 *A young Crahó woman of about sixteen years*

She has the typical Crahó two-sided crown haircut worn by both sexes. The earlobes of the women are not perforated. Indian women marry early, and wives of fourteen or fifteen years of age are not uncommon. Occasionally a man takes a little girl as a wife, but only symbolically; he will first bring her up, and then begins the real married life. The Crahós practice monogamy. In former years it was important that a girl enter marriage as a virgin; a chaste life was also expected of young men. Today these usages, because of the influence of the whites, are no longer adhered to. However, even now the seduction of a young girl is condemned in a court session. In such a proceeding, the village chief does not participate. It is the concern of the kin of the girl. The mother and the maternal relatives stand up as accusers on one side, while the accused is supported by several friends and representatives of the 'Council of Elders.' It is hoped that the seducer will declare himself ready to marry the girl. If not, he must compensate the mother, the aunts, the grandmother, and the males on the maternal side. The girl does not receive any kind of compensation. The father does not participate in such a court session. He stands among the many spectators. In contrast, extramarital sexual relationship is common and is partly regulated by prescribed customs and encouraged. At certain ceremonial hunts and a good many other affairs of a social nature, there is an exchange of spouses. Jealousy by married couples among Crahó Indians is strongly frowned upon. A jealous husband or wife is laughed at by the village community.

3 *A Suyá man with a lip disk*

The Suyás have always inspired fear in the Indian tribes of the upper Xingu region in Central Brazil, but since the end of 1959, they have been living in peace with Indians and whites.

The most striking feature in the appearance of the Suyá male is the large wooden disk worn by married men in the perforated and very much enlarged lower lip. After a Suyá marries, at the time of the ripening of the maize, a feast is prepared during which the underlip of the newly married man is perforated. At first there is inserted a small peg, and after a time this is replaced by larger ones, until a neatly carved and polished disk, such as the one shown in the picture can be worn. The edges of the disk are bent forward, so that the margin of the lip does not slip off.

The wooden disk is worn until old age, but if the margin of the lip becomes enlarged, a new disk is prepared from time to time, and is carefully adjusted, so that it fits tightly and is perfectly balanced.

When the Suyá goes to the nearest stream to bathe, he takes his lip disk out, washes and scrubs the margin of his lip, cleans the lip disk, and inserts it again. The upper side of the lip disk is painted bright red, while the underside is coated with white chalk and decorated with dark delicate patterns.

These lip disks are worn by the Suyás even at night. The Indians do not indulge in kissing. However, this wooden disk hinders the wearer as far as eating and drinking are concerned. Solid food is pushed into the mouth in small morsels. In order to drink, the vessel must be pushed between the lips and the fluid drained into the mouth by the tongue, a procedure which would be miserable for us.

In order to smoke, the pipe or cigar must be pressed into the farthest corner of the mouth, where it is wedged so that the necessary contact between the lips and the cigar takes place.

The constant presence of the wooden lip disk against the lower teeth loosens them, so that older men frequently have teeth bent inward.

The earlobes of the Suyás are perforated. The men wear links made of spiraled strips of palm leaves. The Indians have a very slight facial hair growth. Some of the Suyá men have a thin mustache, but for the most part the Indians remove the beard, eyebrows, and eyelashes.

4 *and* 5 *Javahé man and woman*

The tribal mark of the Javahé and Carajá Indians are two circular scars on both cheeks, which are painted black anew every few days. For this purpose the Indians use the juice of the genipa fruit, which is colorless, but in drying becomes blue-black, and there is no way of removing it for days.

This scar tattooing is performed on boys and girls, and may have something to do with marriage or the reception of those concerned into the society of adults and full fledged membership in the tribe.

In the past, the execution of the circles was accomplished by pressing a wooden pipe on the cheeks, and the deep incision was made with a splinter of rock flint. Today they use a coin to draw the circles and a glass splinter to make the incision. But the use of the tribal mark is still continued.

The other dark facial decorations which appear around the mouths of both Javahés are simple painting made with the above mentioned fruit juice and are not tattooing.

In former times the Javahé and Carajá men went around nude. The women wore a loincloth made of bast; today they still wear it under their clothing and it is made of cotton. Men are now wearing shirts and trousers, just like their Brazilian neighbors.

The Javahé man, above (Picture 4), wears a knitted cotton shawl which is a product of women's skill. At both ends there is a lengthy rounded tissue which is tied together. The Indian uses it as a shawl to cover his shoulders in inclement weather, or to roll himself up in during the night. It can become very cool on the sandbanks of the Araguaya River and on the savanna.

Such knitted cotton shawls are seldom seen among the two tribes. Now the Indians sleep on straw mats under mosquito netting made of cheep cotton, and they cover themselves with cotton cloth for which they trade the Brazilians crocodile hides, dried fish, and feather ornaments. Garlands and glass beads are also obtained in trade.

Both sexes wear their hair long. The man in the picture has cut his shorter in partial imitation of the whites. But the Javahé woman still wears the traditional hair style, a pointed topknot made with tufts of hair. This kind of hairdress was formerly also worn by men, and is still to be seen, especially at certain festive occasions. Both have dyed their naturally nearly coalblack hair with juice and have rubbed it in with palm nut oil to make it deeply black and shining.

6 Robkutsho is one of the song leaders in the Crahó Indian village of Kenpokrekateye

His Brazilian name is Antonio. He is an industrious worker who cultivates a large field. He is also a successful hunter. Both occupations are necessary in order to support his large family. Two of his daughters are already married, and he has several grandchildren. His eyes betray the lasting tension of the Indian who is brought up to observe his surroundings and approach them critically and mistrustfully, always ready for the unexpected and to understand and master whatever comes to pass, good or bad. His face also reflects the simplicity and unselfishness of his character, something which is valued by all Indians. The gentle wisdom of age is highly praised, but young people are also expected to show self-control.

The pock-marked face impresses one with its strength, endurance, and good sense. It is the face of a real human personality.

7 A Young Crahó woman washes her hands

Body cleanliness differs individually. Indians who live near lakes and watercourses, usually wash several times a day. The women take along their pots and other kitchen utensils, put them in the water, then enjoy themselves swimming and diving, while thousands of tiny fish remove the remainder of the food. Then the scrubbing with sand and the washing become easier. Indians clean their hair and bodies carefully with sand and water. The beauty culture actually begins with the careful staining of the body and face with earth and plant dye. The color may be white, brown, red-yellow, or black. The favorites are red and black.

Ritualistic ablutions are often performed. During the ceremonial dances, women pour water from calabashes on the participants. During the major ritualistic war games between the same tribes, the 'Bees' (one of the dances of the participating teams) attack the 'Polecats,' who put on a sham defense. In this pantomime, the Bees carry burning torches and storm at the Polecats with great howls. In order to repulse the attack, the Polecats close ranks. Behind them are rows of women who pour water from their calabashes over their bodies, and extinguish the flaming torches. The consequence is that the stinger of the Bees, which the flames had let loose, can do no harm. No one is touched with the torches for it is a purely symbolic performance.

Before the initiation of the chiefs, there are ritualistic ablutions, and after attending a funeral the Crahó wash themselves throughly, pouring water on each others' naked bodies in the house of mourning. In this picture Crantot is washing her hands with water which she has taken in her mouth. This was done before fetching food for the author which was prepared with the hands.

8 A Maku girl gives a bath to her little brother

Time and again one finds among Indians little girls taking care of their younger brothers and sisters. They carry them on the hip, the way we ride children on the shoulder. They play with them, feed them, wash and bathe them, and this gives the mother more time to devote to the well-being of the family, for it is necessary for her to work all day. She must cook, clean, weave, spin, make pottery, and perform many other tasks of every day living, which are as much a part of Indian housekeeping as they are elsewhere.

The girl is bathing the child inside the hut by simply pouring water over him from a calabash, painted black inside, which keeps it from rotting. The color of the hair of young children is often brown, and occasionally it is quite blond, later it becomes progressively darker. Girls wear a string around their hips, as well as under the knee, which signifies that the girl is clothed. The tightly bound string around the ankles of the baby is for the purpose of development of strong leg muscles.

The girl wears a necklace of glass beads, a gift of the author. The little boy wears a necklace of teeth. Animal teeth have symbolical meaning among many Indian tribes. Crocodile teeth are supposed to possess magical power to ward off evil spells. Jaguar teeth endow the wearer with courage and strength, especially if the wearer has killed the jaguar himself, and it adds to the respect for the hunter in Indian society. Indians do not wear shoes. Children become accustomed early to running barefoot through the thorny forests. They learn to avoid the thorns, seeming to take no heed as to where they step, and yet keep clear of everything that might hurt their feet. In the course of the years, a protective, thick, and very hard horny sole is formed.

9 Crahó Indian woman: mother and child

The birth of a child is always an event in an Indian village. The parents are so strongly tied to the newborn that they feel their behavior will have a direct influence on the well-being of the child. The parents frequently must undergo abstention from food and the fast may last days or even weeks. They must not eat food which they think may harm the child. For example, some Indians abstain from eating the meat of the howling monkey, because it is an animal that moves slowly and has a dark, ugly coat, therefore the child could become slow-moving and develop a dark skin. In contrast, they partake of the meat of the deer, for its fleetness and nimbleness are supposes to help the child. They also eat the piranha, a predatory fish, whose abominable deeds are told in many books, because it represents strength and aggressiveness. These usages, however, differ in the various tribes, depending upon their beliefs.

Both parents love their children very much, but among many tribes the brother of the wife has the responsibility for the raising and guidance of the child in the tribal traditions and duties.

Indian children are nursed a long time. It may happen that a child is still sucking its mother's breast after another infant has arrived.

This picture illustrates the absence of eyebrows and eyelashes, for they have been carefully removed. The features are Mongoloid and sometimes the well known Mongolian spot can be seen on children.

The infant wears a bracelet of grass seed, which may have magical significance. The mother gladly puts on the child all kinds of ornaments, which are supposed to protect it against evil.

Among the Umutinas the newborn are rubbed with a mixture of powdered mussel and tortoise shell and oil. This serves to protect the child from the influence of evil coming from the Other World.

10 Umutina boy with arrow

At birth Umutina boys receive from their maternal uncles a small bow and arrows. The father puts away the weapons until his son can accompany him on the hunt. At first he is permitted to carry home small game. Then one day he kills his first small animal, a squirrel or a hare, or even a small monkey. The Indians amuse themselves by the hour practicing archery. It is not merely for the pride of being a better shot, but for the enjoyment of the game, and thus by playing they becomes a master marksmen.

Little Jukuepa wears a neckband made of wildcat teeth which his father gave him. The double strand of human hair is a characteristic ornament of the tribe and probably has magical qualities.

11 Crahó Indians: mother and child, rest on the march

Entire villages of Crahós will often undertake long marches on sunburned or rain-drenched savannas. Sometimes it is a hunt lasting several days, or a fishing expedition in remote and rare savanna streams. On these wanderings mothers take their children along. The youngest child is carried on the breast in a shawl. In former times it was carried in a girdle made of bast. Older children, as seen in the picture, must walk in the Indian manner, single file, one behind another. Any other formation would be impossible in the wilderness.

The Indians marching in this manner can also carry on conversation, for they are used to it. Each marcher follows in the footsteps of the one ahead of him, and this serves as a protection against snakes which are not infrequently encountered during the rainy season. If one of the children on the march becomes tired, the father, uncle, or an older brother takes pity on it and carries it for a little while on his shoulders. But for the most part the women on the march are accompanied by few men. The men hunt in the undergrowth and primeval forest. This is done so that there will be meat for the campfire, when the women begin to serve the flat cakes which they have baked.

The Crahó Indians very seldom travel continuously for more than three or four miles, since the women, children, and aged of the tribe accompany them. The Chief of the Village decides upon the next campsite on the march.

The mother is always friendly, and her young ones learn all the things of daily life in their play. At an early age they go to the water source, fill the bottle gourds, and carry them home. They gather firewood accompanied by their mother or an older sister. The little girls help with the household duties and still have enough time left to play.

The children are for the most part willing and obedient. If they are not, they are punished, not by being struck, but through milder yet effective means. If a child is disobedient, he is ignored and overlooked for the time being, as if he did not exist. Pretty soon he will follow the good rules of Indian life.

12 A Cashináua boy licks wild honey

The Brazilian Indians originally did not have sugar. Only a few Indian tribes set out sugar cane, which was introduced late by the whites. The scarcity of sugar is met largely by the use of wild honey, but there are not enough bees to permit the daily enjoyment of honey. Many species of bees are to be found in the forests and savannas. For every one of them the Indian has a designation.

Strange as it may seem, the wild bees in Brazil have no sting. Only wasps and hornets are provided with stingers, and they seldom have more than a small quantity of honey in their nests. The wild bees have their nests in hollow trees, in which they build globular structures hanging down from branches and tree trunks, or forming wide passageways upward on very large tree trunks.

Some of the species attack humans who try to take their honey. They bite furiously, get themselves entangled in great numbers in the long hair of their assailants and pinch it off. In order to protect themselves, the Indians light large straw torches, smoke out the bees, and as a consequence the entire bee swarm perishes. Before a honey gathering expedition, certain Indian tribes organize a ceremony. They appeal to the protective spirit of the bees by singing. They ask his permission to take out the honey, or they try to persuade the protecting spirit to cause the honey to be thick and sweet and not watery and tasteless. The taste of wild honey differs greatly, depending on the kind, and the time of the year it is gathered. The honey of the favorite tiuba bees is sweet and thick; other species of bees yield sweetish peppery-tasting honey, or even honey with a sourish taste. The Umutinas told the author that the eating of a certain kind of honey causes a transitory state of insanity.

Honey is seldom stored, it is eaten immediately after being gathered. It is divided up, and a part of it is mixed with water and made into a beverage. Beeswax is used for making figurines. Mixed with a resinous substance, it is employed in making arrows and other objects of daily use.

13 A Cashináua drinks maize soup from a calabash

The best known drink of the Indians is the so-called 'chicha', a designation that does not apply generally to all Indian drinks, but denotes a type of Indian beverage made of ground maize, mandioca roots, ground nuts, bananas, hearts of palm, and other ingredients. Some of these drinks go through a process of fermentation. This happens either because of the addition of mushroom-flavored flat cakes containing certain articles of food, or because the ground and boiled mass is chewed thoroughly by girls and women and then put back in the container with the appropriate beverage. The containers with the beverages which are 'doctored' in this manner are usually put away for several days. The fermentation that follows cannot possibly yield any considerable alcoholic content. Most of the Indian tribes prefer unfermented drinks. Among the Crahó I saw no other liquid used but water, which is obtained from the crystal-clear, cool, clean brooks of the savanna. The Tucunas of the upper Amazon mix the juice of crushed pineapple with water and offer this sweet and aromatic drink to the visitor...

14 Crahó boy drinking water from a halved calabash

Calabashes are the same as bottle gourds. They are the fruit of creeping vines that the Indians put out in their fields. According to the species to which they belong, the fruit are of various sizes and forms. There are large round calabashes, and long ones that bulge in the middle and look like bottles. After they ripen, the skin becomes as hard as wood, and all of them contain seeds. Those used are the matured and hardened fruit which are divided exactly in half by the Indians.

The calabash plant was imported from Africa and is very much liked, because it is not an annual as the bottle gourd is.

Its fruit is almost globular and is all of about the same size. The green fruit is cut and the white, soft pulp, which fills the entire fruit, is removed. After it is dried the skin becomes firm and hard. But the original calabashes are still planted in great numbers and are in daily use. They are used for drinking and for the distribution of sticky liquid foods, for the preservation of food and the gathering of fruit, as well as many other purposes.

15 *A Carajá woman cooks*

Carajá women cook daily in earthen pots of their own making. The favorite dish of their tribe is called kalogi. It consists of starchy meal mixed with water till it becomes a pulpy, glassy liquid which is eaten with everything: with boiled and baked food, with fried fish and smoked meat, with steamed turtle meat and dried turtle eggs. A Carajá Indian is dissatisfied with his meal if no kalogi is served.

The Indians are not familiar with mixed dishes. They prepare all food articles separately – maize, sweet potatoes, mandioca roots, calabash, beans, fruits, and tubers from the forest. The only seasoning is pepper.

Though Carajá women now wear calico dresses, their kitchens are still situated in the open on the wonderful white, soft, and practically endless sandbanks of the Araguáya River in Central Brazil. This woman wears metal rings on her fingers, which she has obtained from the traders, but in her kitchen she prepares only dishes that are in accordance with the old traditions of the tribe. Western civilization has touched the Carajá Indians only superficially. Their food, their craftmanship, as well as the mentality and values of the tribe have remained genuinely Indian, and this is true of many other tribes.

16 *Cashináua boy feeds his younger brother mandioca meal*

The hair on his forehead is shaved. In his perforated earlobes one of the children wears an ornamental pendant made of glass pearls at the end of which are threaded seed globules.

17 *Makú women prepare meal from the fruit of the pupunha palm*

The Makú are very primitive Indians. They do not even have little benches or straw mats to squat on when they work; they sit on the bare ground. The woman to the left sits on a piece of tree bark and works on it at the same time. The work tools of the Makú are also very simple. For the purpose of mashing the peeled fruit of the pupunha palm which have been cut into small bits and already cooked, the woman employs a tree root thickly studded with sharp points and hard thorns. To support this grating implement, the woman has pushed a branch under one side and is holding the other end on her thigh. The grated fruit is sifted by the woman on the right. The meal is bright yellow and very fine. It is to be seen in the flat basket on the extreme right. Later it will be mixed with water and cooked in large earthen pots. The result is a souplike, pleasant-tasting brew. After dark, large pots of this dish are placed in the village square. Young and old scoop calabashes full of this drink and lap up mighty portions; thus the pots are soon empty.

18 *Graceful eating*

Modesty while eating is held in high regard by the Indians. There are Indian tribes who consider the fact that they have to eat a cause for shameful emotion. Everyone eats alone, hiding in some corner, turned away from the others. They are ashamed in the same manner as we are ashamed of the necessity for other physiological functions and want to do them in privacy. Even among those Indians who do not regard eating as a shameful act and take their meals together, there are certain regulations as to behavior. These, of course, are known to the members of the tribe and are abided by unconsciously. Thus, for instance, it is taken for granted that one who participates in a meal, whether he uses a wooden spoon or a scoop, will take out of the common pot only small pieces of meat or fish, and cut off small morsels from the roast on the spit.

The Crajó woman in our picture is holding a piece of game roasted on the open fire. She holds it with such grace and beauty of hand gesture, and such charm that the best brought up person could not do any better. At the same time joy shines in her eyes because of the seldom experienced pleasure of eating a small piece of meat. Meat is not by any means a daily food among most Indian tribes.

19 *The making of a large maize bread loaf among the Umutinas*

The Umutinas call the large nearly forty-inchlong maize bread loaf mataricá. The women harvest the ears of corn, remove the husks, and grind the kernels. They sift the still rough meal obtained from the ears of maize, regrind the remaining large pieces of kernels in a mortar, and sift the meal again. The result is a coarse flour. Barucolotó, the woman in the picture, mixes the flour with water and kneads the dough. The man, Atucaré, has built a wood fire. He has also gathered a large bundle of banana leaves. Barucolotó spreads the leaves on a thin mat on the floor of the hut. She puts the dough on it, folds it and ties it up with bast. Then she puts it in the hot ashes of the hearth fire and covers it with tree bark and billets of wood which smoulder all night. Next morning the maize bread is baked brown crisp and tasty. It is the daily food of the Umutina Indians.

20 *The big mandioca meat pie of the Crahó Indians*

The Crahó Indians bake in a manner similar to that of the Umutinas. Their pies, which are prepared for special festive occasions, are seven to ten feet in diameter. The meal of the ground Mandioca roots is spread on a pad of banana leaves. Many small morsels of meat are distributed upon it. The folded leaf parcel is then put on glowing hot stones, covered with old straw mats, a thick layer of palm leaves, and finally with a layer of earth. At the break of day next morning the earth is removed, the partially moist palm leaves and straw mats are taken off, and the baked meat pie is ready to be distributed among all the villagers. This is the national dish of the Crahó.

21 *The Cashináua women gather peanuts*

The peanut is a legume of Indian origin. The nuts grow underground on the roots of suffrutescent plants. They thrive exceptionally well in sand, for they can be advantageously planted at the beginning of the dry season on the banks of streams and lakes, and gathered before the rainy season begins. The Cashináua women carefully pull the plants out of the ground and the nuts remain fastened to the roots.

Among the Cashináua all the women of a village gather the peanuts at the same time. These legumes are packed in baskets and carried into the village by the men and women. There the vines are tied with the leaves into knots and strung on horizontal poles so that the legumes hang down loose. The women shell the peanuts, grind them in mortars and form loaves of hand length.

The Indians also like to make soups and drinks out of the crushed nuts, which taste very good and have important nourishing qualities.

22 *The Cashináua gather bananas*

It is not known whether bananas were to be found on this continent before the discovery of America, or were later brought in. Today one can find bananas being used by almost all Indians, and some tribes are real banana eaters.

There are many kinds of bananas, from dwarfed species to gigantic-sized ones, twenty inches long. There are certain kinds that are used in the preparation of meal, others are roasted green or are mashed and used for the preparation of soup, and finally there is the delicious fruit banana. The Cashináua offer guests a drink made of a sweet kind of banana which has been roasted over a fire and dissolved in water. This is very refreshing and pleasant-tasting. It is considered discourteous to refuse this drink when it is offered, or not to empty the container in one draft.

The planting of bananas among the Cashináua and many other Indian tribes is so extensive that they can collect bananas every day. Other tribes frequently possess only a few plants in their fields. For them bananas are a very rare but highly valued treat. Heavy baskets full of halfripe bananas are dragged home by Cashináua children, as well as by women and men, and hung to ripen. Bananas grow the year round provided there is sufficient moisture. Many Indians arrange for festivities on occasions of banana gathering.

23 *Among the Crahó Indians the woman carries most of the load on marches*

Mats for sitting and sleeping, calabashes, cooking utensils, and foodstuffs must be carried on the back. The man must keep his hands free for the purpose of defending his family and for hunting, but if it becomes necessary, he helps with the load. The woman's carrying girdle rests on the top of her head, not on her forehead. It is not easy to give the probable weight of such a burden; it may reach sixty pounds or even more.

The woman in this picture is an elderly Crahó Indian. She is dressed in a waistcloth. It is made preferably from red cotton material, seven feet long, and is simply wrapped around the body with the ends tucked in.

The little dog is her pet. Later it may develop into a capable sporting dog for the hunting of deer, wild boar, tapirs, pacas, or anteaters. Most Indian dogs are useless curs, but some tribes train their dogs patiently and devotedly and make excellent hunting dogs out of them. When it happens that a good hunting dog of the Crahó, in the pursuit of a deer, falls down a precipice and is killed, loud death laments can be heard in the hut of its owner. It is as if a human being had died.

24 A Crahó hunter with the carcass of a doe

The Crahós are hunters; the oldsters of the tribe relate how plentiful game was in their youth. The men went out into the savanna armed with bow and arrow and club and came back with rich booty. Today the Crahó hunt with muzzle-loaders, and without them a successful hunt is unthinkable The game is scarce and timid. João Creolo was one of the best hunters of his village. He carries a savanna deer, the largest wild deer of the plains. Besides this species of deer, there are also various smaller kinds. A bigger species, notable for its antlers, is found in the marshy regions.

The feet of the killed animal are tied together with strips of young palm leaves. João Creolo has also put strips over his chest and the upper part of his arm. The head of the deer is tied so that it will not hang down and interfere with the movements of the hunter.

The hunter does not eat the game he has killed. If he did, the Crahó believes, he would have no luck on the next hunt. The meat of this deer will be distributed among the relatives of the hunter in accordance with the degrees of kinship. The head and the middle intestines are the favorite parts.

João is dead. He had wavy hair, for one of his ancestors was an African who settled with the Crahó. There are Negro half-breeds among the Crahós, recognizable by their wavy hair. As for the color of their skin and their habits, they do not differ from the other Crahó Indians.

25 and 27 An Umutina woman, Cocolotó (25), and an Umutina man, Atucaré (27), sing in the opening of the death ritual (For a further portrayal of the death ritual see N. 59, 60, 64)

The Umutina women cut their hair very short. The men let theirs grow long and tie it in a knot on the top of the head. Both sexes have their earlobes perforated in early youth, and from the earlobes hang large colored feather tassels. Atucaré's tassels are turned back and tipped over the animal skin that he carries on his back.

Both the man and the woman are decorated with tribal marks which consist of feathers of the curassow. These are evenly placed in a resinous substance and are pasted on the upper arms. On her neck and body Cocolotó wears many strands of animal teeth. The smaller teeth are those of monkeys and coati, the larger ones are those of wild boars. It takes decades to collect so many animal teeth. To begin with, a father may bring home with him from the hunt a couple of teeth for his little daughter, later as a wife she receives from her husband after a successful hunt a few more teeth, which she pierces and strings. In past generations the Umutinas used the teeth of their slain enemies for these necklaces, piercing them with fish teeth. Today they use pointed knives obtained from the white man.

Atucaré also wears a chain made of the canine teeth of a jaguar, the biggest and strongest beast of prey in the central Brazilian primeval forest. The Umutinas are afraid to face the jaguar with only a bow and arrow. The possession of a jaguar necklace is understandably the desire of every young man. Conquered fear is, after all, the test of real courage! Both have strings of human hair wound around their necks. From time to time women permit their hair to grow long in order to prepare for themselves strings of hair many feet long. The man twists them at the beginning of the ceremony for the dead. There is no doubt a magical reason for this custom, but the author could not to his regret, get a full explanation.

The seed chains on Cocolotó's wrists are worn almost entirely for religious ceremonies. Umutina women and girls wear skirts made of woven cotton of their own making. Is is a seamless web, a veritable sack, which, when it is folded over once, is stretched so tightly that it remains firmly on the hip. Atucaré wears a headdress made of red ara feathers. In his perforated lower lip there is inserted a bone peg with a head like that of a nail. On ordinary days he wears a lip plug carved from the root of the small aromatic musacea tree. On Atucaré's back hang the skins of jaguars, wildcats, otters, and monkeys. The Umutinas believe that after death one of the three human souls is embodied in animals, and in these skins is a power capable of facilitating communication with one of these souls.

The bow and arrows of the Umutinas are especially big and heavy. They are proud of their weapons. Atucaré sings in the opening of the ceremonial for the dead. For ritual reasons he keeps his right hand on his throat. In his song he invites the souls of all the dead to participate in the ensuing ceremony. Atucaré sings through the entire night until the dawn, then is relieved by another Umutina. The ceremonies of the dead last for some six weeks.

26 *A young Crahó boy with half-sized wood disks in his perforated earlobes*

The Mongolian shape of the eyes of the boy in this picture can be clearly seen. Some of the Crahó Indians have their teeth filed in points by the witch doctors. Pointed teeth are considered attractive and at the same time filing prevents tooth decay, and parts of teeth affected with caries are removed at once. The point of a big hunting knife is put on the affected part of the tooth. With a strong, short, and accurately aimed blow the witch doctor hits the back of the knife with a small cudgel, and the appropriate part of the tooth is splintered away. The pointing of teeth is to be found among many peoples all over the world.

28 *A Crahó boy with a tame hyacinth ara*

Indians frequently have tame animals. The big blue parrot was the tamest bird in the author's experience in many years of traveling in Brazilian primeval forests. The bird, lying on its back, was petted by the Indian children like a puppy. The captured bird would never make use of his powerful beak, even when the play became quite rough.

The body of the Crahó child has been daubed festively with dark paint. After a few days the paint begins to crack and it does not look very pretty.

29 *A Carajá Indian with a parrot*

Parrots are the most frequent and favorite pets among Indians. Occasionally they are taken out of their nests when they are still devoid of feathers and raised by Indian women with great affection and devotion. Later these domesticated birds and other animals from the forests live perfectly free among their human friends. The birds sleep in the hut or on the roof, or spend nights in the nearby forests. When a domesticated bird or mammal finds a mate, it may return to its real home in the forest for a short time, or permanently. The Umutinas keep tamed birds, because they believe that one of the human souls is embodied in certain animal species after death. Among the Umutinas these soul-carrying birds are a part of the household. They receive plentiful food and they are never given away or sold. When such a bird dies it is buried and given the same kind of funeral, though smaller, as that prescribed for human beings. Nothing can better illustrate the relationship between man and animal among the Indians than this usage.

The Carajá wears a wooden plug in his perforated lower lip; on his cheeks are two painted scartattoos, his tribal mark. The bands he wears on his forearms are made of red dyed crocheted cotton. These are characteristic of the Carajá and their neighbors the Tapirapé.

30 *The catching of the large piracucu fish by Carajá Indians*

The piracucu is the largest scaled fish to be found in the Amazon Basin. In most parts of Brazil, and in other South American countries, the fresh as well as the salted and dried meat of this giant fish forms the foundation of the nourishment of the Indian and civilized population. It has a long lung sac and must come to the surface for air. This is its downfall, for the fishermen hook it with a steel harpoon while it is getting air. Its body is covered with a mantle of large, rough scales. Its long head is bony. No fish, not even the dreaded piranha, is its equal.

The Carajás begin their catching of the piracucu by spreading a large meshed net, some over a hundred and thirty feet long. It is stretched over the surface of connecting tributaries of rivers or lakes. At each end of the net wait two Indians with clubs. Others are stationed at a distance, and as they close in on the net they whip the water with long rods. The piracucu comes up frightened, swims on the surface of the water until it is caught in the wide meshes of the net. A waiting Indian dives in at once, grabs the fish, and hauls it to the surface. Then one of the Indians kills the powerful fish with a club. The delicious meat is always divided equally among all the villagers.

Before starting out on the fishing expedition the Carajás organize a magic ceremony. It is obviously a petition to the lord, or protective spirit of the fish, for successful results. Both Carajá young men wear very long carved lip plugs, which look like narrow neckties. Older men use only short wooden stumps in order to cover the opening in the under-lip.

31 *The shooting of fish with bow and arrows*
The Indians are highly skilled in shooting fish. They practice from early youth. The refraction of light on the water is no obstacle and they seldom miss a shot. Even if the fish are far out in the river, or in a water current where they cannot be hit by a direct flight of an arrow, they catch them anyway. The arrow is sent in a high curve, whizzing at a distance of a hundred feet or more and pierces almost without fail the swiftly gliding fish.

This Carajá boy has made his own bow and arrow. He proudly brought to his mother in the kitchen the fish he caught with his weapons.

32 *In a typical Carajá Indian canoe two large piracucu fish are brought into the village. (These fish are to be found in the summer on the immense, sunbaked sandbanks of the Araguáya River.)*
Indians who are settled around the great rivers and lakes usually have abundant food supplies: fish, turtles, and their eggs, the produce of their fields, an occasional chunk of meat as a result of their hunting, wild honey, tuberous plants from the forests, and fruit.

33 – 36 *Fishing with poison among the Crahó Indians*
There are many varieties of poisons which the Indians use in fishing. The fish caught in this manner are harmless for human consumption. Most of the fish poisons are derived from the liana plants found in the savannas and forests. Some of them paralyze the breathing muscles of the fish, so that they choke to death; others damage the mucus membrane and prevent the fish from escaping.

Bundles of poisonous liana plants are put in the water and are broken up with cudgels. The juice of these plants mixes with the water, and drugs or kills the fish. The Indians kill the dying or injured fish with bow and arrow, and gather them in baskets. In this manner many fish can be obtained. The best time for this kind of fishing is at the end of the dry season when the watercourses are low. In rapidly moving water the poison cannot be employed successfully.

In the savannas of the Crahó Indians there are only a few rivers, and they are rapid flowing streams with few fish in them. Only once or twice a year is a fishing expedition undertaken by one or more villages at the same time. It is a great festival occasion, participated in by young and old alike. Simple huts are put up in the camp (see pictures 35 & 36). Cords are tied together and covered with leaves and branches for temporary use. Here families find sufficient shelter for a few days. The women take care of the preparation of food from supplies they have carried in baskets on their backs.

The men prepare for the fishing. The woman in picture 36 fetches water in a bottle gourd, carrying her child at the same time (picture 34). In front of the house there is a grate, with an even, low-burning fire on which the cleaned fish will be smoked. Picture 35 shows two Suyá girls dragging a gigantic taraira fish, a typical nocturnal fish of prey found in South American rivers. Its meat is highly valued.

37 *After the expedition*
The bowstrings are loosened and the bow and arrow carefully preserved. The bowstring must not remain taut. It is lengthened by letting out the winder. Before the expedition the opposite is done when it is shortened. The Crahó bends the strong bow with his knee and places the loop of the bowstring on the top of the bow. This keeps the bow ready for use. Bow and arrow are the typical weapons of the Indians and are to be found among all tribes, although there are some who prefer the blowgun for hunting.

The making of a bow is men's work and requires much knowledge and manual skill. The trunks of various palm trees, and also other timber, are used. Some bows made of palm trunks are polished after they have been completed and are as black and shining as ebony. The string is made of strips of palm leaf shoots or twisted out of bast. While the bows are being made they are frequently soaked in water so that the wood does not dry up or crack. If an Umutina Indian has no luck hunting with a new bow, he cuts it into equal halves and presents them to his wife, who uses them as digging sticks in planting or for gathering roots in the forest.

During the ritual for the dead, which the Umutinas call

Boku, the Bow Festival, all the bows of the tribe are gathered in a huge pile, tied together, and at the dance ceremony consecrated to one of the ancestors to whom this festival is dedicated.

Indian bows do not shoot very far. An accurately aimed shot at a hundred and seventy feet distance is considered a good accomplishment. The arrows, of course, fly much farther and may cause mortal injury.

There are various kinds of arrows: single and double-hooked, with a dull point for bird hunting; with several points for fishing; with daggerlike points for big game and war; and others, such as poisonous and nonpoisonous, according to their purpose.

38 *A Javahé woman with her body painted for the fertility dances of her tribe. (For a more detailed description of the fertility dance see numbers 65, 69, 74)*

The everyday apparel of Javahé and Carajá Indian women is simple clothing. But when in the summer the Aruanã, the fertility dances, are staged on the hot, soft white sandbanks, the participating girls and women adorn themselves in accordance with the customs of their forebears. The long blue-black hair is combed and freshly oiled. The hair on the crown of the head is made into a small topknot which stands erect. A new bast apron is made and is wrapped around the body and drawn through the legs.

The body is decorated with the juice of green gempa fruit in continuously repeated geometrical designs. They are the same patterns that are found on paddles, mortars, lances, and other Javahé objects. It is possible that they have some connection with the soft elastic stride of these people. In one myth it is related that out of the movement of duck's feet the paddle originated. The Indian men and women do not tread heavily either on the soft sand nor on the hard ground. There is an extra-ordinary beauty in the proud movement of the Indian body, which is expressed in the harmony and grace of this Javahé woman. When their feet sink slightly into the sand, there can be heard a sound like low singing.

39–41 *Cashináua Indians on fishing expedition with poison*

The Cashináua live on the upper course of the Curanja, which flows into one of the tributaries of the mighty Amazon. During the rainy season these upper courses become raging mountain streams. In the dry season they contain so little water that the Indians use them as paths. In the remaining lagoons, and in certain stretches of water, there are large numbers of fish.

The Cashináuas plant not far from their houses a quick and powerfully acting fish poison. The green leaves are plucked by the women, mashed in special wooden mortars which are not used for the grinding of food, and then stored in baskets.

After the mashed leaves have gone through a fermentation process and turned black, the Cashináua go up the river for several days until they reach the rapids. The dip the baskets with the fish poison (picture 40) into the water. In seconds the fish are poisoned in the calm water. When in a silvery glittering mass they attempt to jump out of the water, it looks like fireworks. The smaller fish are quickly stupefied or die and the big ones attempt to escape. The Cashináua pursue them, shouting, with bows and arrows and capture a great many. Upon their return to the village the great catch is celebrated joyfully with a dance.

The man in picture 40 carries in his bast belt a steel knife, which he received in trade from the author in exchange for a beautiful handmade object.

42 *A Cashináua Indian – fire driller*

Matches have found the long way through the primeval forest, and only the Indians living in very distant areas still use a fire driller. Furthermore the Indians do not permit the fire in the hearth to go out if they can help it. If it happens, however, glowing coals are contributed by a neighbor. Matches become damp and cannot be used, but with the fire driller one can build a fire under any weather conditions. There are various kinds of fire drillers. The one in our picture is the most common. A wide bamboo strip is placed on two pieces of wood. On the floor lies a small ball of cotton. The upright round staff, a branch of the Urucu bush, or an arrow in case of necessity, is turned with both hands and at the same time pressed down on the bamboo strip. This strip has, from former fire-making twirlings, round blackish spots that can be seen clearly.

Through friction and turning the upright stave penetrates the support. Heat is generated; at first there is a little smoke and suddenly a spark is thrown off and falls on the bunch of cotton on the floor. The Cashináua blows carefully on the tiny flame and feeds it small sticks. Soon the flame is big and strong, and can be fed kindling. The Cashináuas take their fire equipment wrapped up in leaves wherever they go. They do not as yet know the miracle of the match, the miracle that fails whenever nature is covered with moisture.

43 *A Makú fits out arrows for his blowgun with curare poison*

Not all Indians are familiar with arrow poison, but the small arrows from the blowgun must be equipped with powerfully acting poison if they are to have lethal effect. The weight of such an arrow is not sufficient to kill game. The most used poison is curare. Its particular effect comes from certain strychnic plants. Only where these plants are to be found in the primeval forest is it possible for the Indian to prepare effective arrow poison. The recipe for the curare is a vigilantly kept secret. Not all members of the tribe know it. The one who prepares it must undergo fasting and certain dietary restrictions and carry out certain magical acts. Besides the poison, the Indian poisoned arrow is equipped with ballast. The Makús often prepare little arrows for their blowguns. First of all, the little arrows are treated with the poison. Then they are laid out on two tree trunks lying side by side on the floor, so that the thin fluid of the poison may be dried in the sun. In the next few days elliptical balls made of thread from the pods of the cotton plant are attached to them. The finished arrows are tied into a small bundle and shoved into the straw roof of the hut. Children and adults handle these dangerously poisoned weapons rather carelessly. It is not known whether accidents have taken place or whether there is an antidote.

44 *The handling of a blowgun by Makú Indians*

Blowguns are about four to ten feet long, depending on the tribe to which the user belongs. The picture illustrates the accustomed position of the blowgun when it is in use. The blowgun is smoothly and evenly hollowed out, so that the arrow can glide through it easily and hold the exact direction in which it was aimed.

The cheek muscles of the blowgun shooter are expanded in bullet shape. Then he draws the muscles tightly together and forces the collected air through the gun. There is a hissing, squeaky noise and the little arrow with its poisoned point leaves the bore with great speed. It is sufficient to wound the game only lightly, the fragile point remains easily stuck, and the paralyzing poison quickly does its work. The aim is so certain that a Makú, for instance, can hit a bird of the size of a pigeon at a distance of a hundred and thirty feet.

There are blowguns which, besides the mouthpiece that makes possible the connection between the mouth of the shooter and the blowgun, also have an attachment for facilitating the aim – one or two aguti teeth are fastened to the shaft, and also serve for taking bearings.

In order to make a blowgun, the Makús fit two matched reeds and insert them in each other. Other Indians use two half lengths, fit them carefully together, and wrap them into one rod. Monkeys, wild boar, tapirs, deer, and birds are easily shot. The Indians prefer their silent blowguns to our noisy firearms. The curare arrow poison can also be lethal as far as human beings are concerned. It is used for all kinds of medical purposes, among others for a particular narcosis.

45 *Wrestling among Carajás and Javahés*

When wrestling matches are to be held, groups from different villages visit each other. Canoes full of young fellows paddle for hours up or down the river. From the afternoon until late at night wrestling matches take place between the home boys and the visitors. In every Carajá and Javahé village there is to be found one Indian who has a reputation of being the strongest and best wrestler. The Indians amuse themselves when wrestling matches are organized by seeing to it that the champion is always challenged by a new opponent until he is so worn out that even the oldest and weakest of the villagers can throw him. He then becomes the laughingstock of all present. This is genuine Indian humor. The rules of the wrestling matches are similar to ours: whosoever's back touches the sand has lost the match.

46–49–50 *The ritualistic foot races of the Crahó Indians*

In the early afternoon the Crahós organize daily foot races in which the participants carry logs. These logs are carved from buriti palm trunks and weigh up to two hundred pounds. The two teams compete with one another. When a racer tires, a fresh man is available to take the log upon his shoulder. The starting point of the race is five-eights of a mile to two miles away from the village, on specially built clean and straight roads that lead directly into the village. Every team has an honor virgin as its honorary member who, at the closing feast of the summer and winter log races, plays a very important role.

Every day the sports leader invites the teams to competition by loud singing. When the sun reaches a certain point in the heavens, his melodious voice is heard in the village. The team assembles at once at his house, or runs out to the assembling place on the savanna. Two new buriti palm logs have already been prepared by two Crahós for the race. The Crahós have a high standard of physical fitness and all strive for bodily development, for young fellows who are unable to perform athletically are despised. As far as we know, the competition with large and heavy logs serves only for the development of athletic fitness, but small, light, hollowed logs represent the souls of the dead, and thus there may be a connection between these races and the religious concepts of the tribe.

The national sport of the Crahós, log running, is tied up with the tribe's mythology. Sun and Moon, two men, were the first Crahó Indians in the world. After the daily hunt they organized a log race for themselves, and the sport was passed on to their descendants, the present-day Crahós. On special occasions there are also races by female teams, but the logs they carry are somewhat lighter than those carried by the men.

47–48 *Indian boys playing*
The life of Indian children is natural, happy, and unburdened. Harmonious relations among children is an outstanding characteristic. Differences of opinion arise, but they never result in loud disputations or fights. The day is long, and youth enjoys much freedom. Even when children help their parents fetching water, on the hunt, fishing or gathering honey, these occupations form a part of the brimful joy of the young. In the summer there is heard the merry laughter of youth on the beach and in the field.

48 *Climbing the pole*
In order to climb a pole, which is placed in the middle of the village square, the boys wrap bast strings around their feet. This performance is derived from one of the important rituals of the Crahó Indians. They plant their bare soles against the pole and squeeze the bast strings, which enables them to swish up the tree trunk or the palm.

51–54 *The hunt*
Hunting is a strenuous occupation. The savannas and forests in South America were never rich in game. Hunting is also the fulfillment of the hunter. Not every animal is considered game. Religious conceptions may restrain an Indian tribe from killing certain animals they believe to be related to them. There exists a guardian spirit of wild boars and other animals, whose permission must be asked before organizing a hunt to kill the animal in question. The favorite game are mammals and wild birds. Monkeys (Picture 51) are considered a delicacy. Among them is the whistling monkey, which most often is killed with bow and arrow.

(52) *The Brazilian land turtle appears in all the Northern regions of Brazil*
A variety with red spots on the head and limbs is to be found in the forest. There is also a turtle with yellow spots in the savanna. At the beginning of the dry and hot season several of these turtles hide together in holes in the ground. The Crahós know these hiding places and are able to take out as many as four, five, or more turtles. The eggs of the land and water turtles are also eagerly gathered and eaten.

(53) *Distribution of the game*
Among the Crahós, as well as among other Indian tribes, the booty of the hunters is distributed to all of the villagers. First they spread palm leaves on the ground – for cleanliness – then the available meat is cut into many small pieces. All present, including widows, orphans, sick hunters, and so on, receive their share.

(54) *A hunting expedition*
The entire village of the Cashináua set out on a several days expedition up the river Curanja, in order to reach new hunting grounds. Every afternoon well before sundown huts were put up in which to spend the night. Ordinary staves were driven forklike into the ground, tied on top with bast,

and covered with palm leaves. From the thin posts swing the hammocks in which the tired hunters will rest. On the grate are fish, game, green bananas, and ears of corn for the evening meal. Every family builds such an overnight shelter for itself and leaves it the next morning.

55 An Urukú Indian woman finds a little wild pig
On hunting expeditions it often happens that mother animals with young are killed. The Indian women take care of the helpless young with affection. They chew up food and squirt it into the mouths of the helpless wild animals. They even breast-feed them until these new household pets become used to humans. They are tied with bast ropes, but soon they run around free everywhere and follow their new masters, who consider them as their equals on hunts, during work in the fields, on deer stalking and far marches. They have become inseparable friends, and the Indians love their domesticated animals very much.

56 The song leader of the Crahó
The most important musical instrument of the Brazilian Indian is the gourd rattle. The song leader of the Crahós, who is at the same time the conductor of the youth in the male and female choirs, gives the pitch for the singing and dancing. If he changes the rhythm of the rattle, it signifies to the singers that he is introducing a new song. Without a break the singers join in the tune. The song leader of the Crahós receives from the people the highest respect. He is frequently also the composer of new verses and music, which are incorporated into the great song treasury of the tribe. If the leader has thought up a new song, he comes to the village square in the evening, and is soon surrounded by young girls and women to whom he sings it. Following this, he forms a group of four women and repeats the song, and all of them learn it. If a song leader's son has the inclination, he may follow his father's occupation. It is always an office of honor. But a song leader must, in addition work his own specialty, go hunting and carry out the various tasks like any other Indian.
The Crahós relate that they are descended from the sun and moon who were humans. The village population is divided into the sun and moon halves. Each of these halves has its own rattle, which seemingly differs only in the number of bored holes.

Among many Indian tribes the rattle is an instrument that reestablishes contact between reality and the world of the spirits. It is frequently of great significance that certain seed kernels are inside to make the rattling noise. In ceremonies with such rattles, it is usually the medicine man who makes use of it. Robcutsho's face and body are decorated festively with red Urukú paint. The black is rubber juice, which is rubbed in with charcoal. One can see clearly his pendulous perforated earlobes in which young fellows wear large colorfully painted or white wooden discs. The thin strips of palm leaves around the forehead and throat are festive ornaments, possibly of magical origin.

57 The village clown dances with young people
These boys have just completed the ceremony of youth initiation and have become full-fledged members of the tribe. Their bodies are rubbed with liquid rubber and covered with down. They now belong to the lowest age category of the village. There are altogether four age categories, and the Council of Elders is selected from the oldest, although not everyone reaches this stage in his life.
After the completion of the festivities, the clown took up with the young people. He started out with a gay rhythmical hip dance. The village Clown has the task of amusing the villagers with his pranks and helping them to while away their time.
Suddenly the loud voice of the chief is heard, announcing the latest news, but in reality it is the clown who is attempting to create excitement. It is all in fun. During the collective activity and celebration he engages in teasing the women until they become exasperated and drive him away by hitting him with soft palm leaves. Frequently his jokes are not very proper – but here it is a matter of a gay dance that provides joy for the youth and is soon ended.

58 Joyful dance around the circular-shaped village
It is late in the afternoon. Some men and women have worked in the field, others have been busy at home. A fine, deep, soft sand covers the road that runs around the circular-shaped Crahó village. On the outside of the village circle are the houses (see picture 57).
Something is always happening in the village! The people

work, or run a race, or have a dance. A couple steps out of a house, loud calls can be heard, they grasp each other. A second pair hurries up and joins the first couple. They move and dance. One leg forward, one backward, two steps forward, one step back. They dance around the village, their faces turned toward the houses. They stop at every house. They sing, call other young people to join the dancing, and soon there is formed a row of rhythmically moving couples, which winds around the circular village. An expression of the pure joy of life!

59–60 *The mask dance of the Umutinas, at the ritual of the dead (See also 25, 27, and 64)*

The Indians have many dances of deep religious significance. Every year the Umutinas organize eighteen ritual dances, which vary in their fancy costumes, presentations, songs, and meaning, but collectively they represent the closed complex of the death ritual. Only kinsmen of the dead who have helped to bury the departed may be masked. Such disguised persons receive, during the six-week duration of the death ritual, the soul of the deceased one, and are for themselves and for those present no longer themselves, but actually the embodied soul of the dead. After each ritual the host of the feast permits the female relatives to gather up the straw that was used in the preparation of the disguises, out of which they weave mats that may be used for reclining, sleeping, or for wrapping up the dead at the funeral.

The Umutinas' belief in resurrection is associated with these straw mats. The Savior Haipuku created men by wrapping up fruit in straw mats. The Sun and the Moon, two friends, have had many adventures together, in which the less capable Moon perished, but his friend the Sun (a man) wrapped up the mortal remains of the Moon in a straw mat, and soon the Moon came back to life.

(59) The host of the feast is squatting down on a straw mat, while two gigantic Hatori masks threaten his eyes with pointed arrows. They approach him, but soon back away without doing him any harm.

(60) Their bodies completely painted black, carrying jaguar skins on their backs, feather ornaments and turbanlike wrappers on their heads, the two men are dancing, deeply immersed in the religious rite. They wave long hunting knives in time with their song. During the ritual of the dead,

they are no longer themselves, because the souls of their kin have possessed them.

61 *Dance of the Cashináua*

After a successful fish-catching expedition, the Cashináua perform a dance that is an expression of pure satisfaction. It can be seen in the faces of the dancers, in the feather ornaments and body paint, in striking contrast to the dramatic buildup and occurrences of the ritual of the dead of the Umutinas (above).

62 *A monkey mask from the virgin initiation of the Tukunas*

The mask is made of bast material drawn over wickerwork. In the mouth opening are teeth of a Brazilian hare, fastened with a resinous substance. The forehead and chin are covered with a layer of black resin. The white stripes are painted with alum. The bast fringe around the head represents hair.

63 *Jaguar effigy from the virgin initiation of the Tukunas*

This effigy is made of white bast material and stands taller than a man. The twig teeth with bloody points indicate that here is the representation of a cannibalistic spirit. But the behavior of the jaguar effigy, which represents the king beast of the Brazilian forests, is depicted by the Tukunas in a very humorous way. To the friendly greetings of the father of the girl whose maturity feast was being celebrated, the jaguar answered in the whining tones of a small child. It contributed to the general jollity of all present.

64 *The ritual of the dead of the Umutina, the dance of the Jurima masqueraders (see description 25, 27)*

The oldest woman of the tribe is kneeling before a masqueraded figure in which is embodied the soul of her departed husband. She strokes the bare feet and weeps as she whispers endearments and sings the death lament over her husband.

The masqueraders, who represent the spirits, have combed their own hair over their faces. Older men, whose hair is no longer sufficient for that purpose, construct wigs for this dance, which is dedicated to the protective spirit of the fish, Jurima. The masqueraded figures carry in their hands palm leaf stalks, from which straw symbols are suspended that represent various kinds of fish. The only one to be seen is to the right in one pattern – a round disk that represents a small edible fish, the pacu.

65 *Aruanã masqueraded figures dance during the summer on the sandbanks*

In the summer there are always clear blue skies that vault over the extensive sandbanks of the Araguaya River of central Brazil. This is the time for the fertility dances of the Javahé and Carajá.

These are religious festivities and the pictured masquerade is one of many different kinds, which represent the souls of animals. In an old myth it is related that the pirarucu fish emerged from the water and for a time lived among the Indians. When the fish returned to their own element, the Indians imitated them in masquerade. The headpiece of the Aruaña mask is made of colored feathers with long bast fringes. The skirt of the costume is of dyed black bast. Large round mother-of-pearl disks on the headpiece represent the eyes. These religious masks of the Javahé and Carajá are under no circumstances turned over to outsiders.

This is a collective description of pictures 62, 63, 66, 67, 72, 73, 86. Virgin initiation among the Tucunas on the Upper Amazon
As soon as there appears in a Tucuna girl the first sign of maturity, she must go into a small retreat in the parent's house to be alone for several weeks. The girl must spend the time industriously spinning and performing other kinds of work. When men are present in the house, she must not under any circumstances leave the place of concealment. At this time of her life, the girl is in constant danger of being destroyed by the evil spirits. Therefore the parents must prepare a great feast and invite many friends and relatives, in whose presence the most important and dangerous features of the initiation are to be carried out.

The father goes out to hunt and fish, then smokes the game for the guests. The mother and relatives prepare enormous vessels of fermented drink. Day and night is heard sounds of the drum and the singing. There is dancing and drinking. Some of the guests have brought with them masks that represent spirits. At one time, the evil spirit attacked some Tucunas and sucked out their blood. The guests' masks are symbolical representations of the cannibal spirits. All of a sudden these masks appear, they come out of the nearby

woods, and engage in a feigned attack on the hiding place of the girl. The attack is repulsed by the guests in a playful defense.

On the third evening after the beginning of the festivities the girl is adorned and led out of the retreat. Now she must carry out a baffling task. The medicine man hands her a glowing splinter, which she must throw at her archenemy who is embodied in a tree. It does not make any difference whether she hits it or not. Having performed this deed, she is free. No evil spirit can any longer do her harm.

At the end of the festivities, the women and the girls assemble and begin to tear out her hair, until all of it is removed from her head. This act signifies symbolically the death of the maid and the resurrection, or the birth, of the young woman. She now becomes marriageable. The virgin initiation is the outstanding event in the life of a Tucuna woman.

66 *Virgin initiation among the Tucunas*

For the first time after many weeks the girls have left the seclusion hut in order to be adorned for the coming festivity. The relatives paint their bodies with the colorless juice of the genipa plant, which, after drying, assumes a deep blue-black color. An ornate headdress with feather decorations and ornaments of glass beads complete the adornment.

In the long stay in the hiding place where they have sat and worked for weeks, the girls were so weakened that they could not stand on their feet without assistance.

This picture portrays a rare double feast. Two girls, cousins on their father's side, are undergoing together the greatest and most significant celebration of their lives.

67 *Virgin initiation among the Tucunas*

The final ceremony of the Virgin initiation consists of pulling out the girl's long hair. She is seated for this purpose on a specially made mat. The women, mostly kin, start with energy to pull out some hair in small bunches. It is a painful procedure. If a girl cries out, a rare occurrence, she receives intoxicating beverages. By rubbing in lemon juice, the hairs are supposed to be loosened and removal is less painful. The long strands and wisps are dyed red. The last hairs are pulled out with a loud joyous shout by the mother's brother, then the final ceremony of the Virgin initiation is ended.

The girl's hair is stored under the straw roof at the entrance of the house.

68 *The Umutinas put on their ornaments for the coming ritual of the dead*

In the masking house, straw mats are spread on the ground. The old Yarepá wears on his forehead a head ornament made of the long feathers of eagles' wings, held in place by a hair roll that looks like a round black brush. The straw of young buriti palm leaves is wound under the arms and legs. The body is decorated with luminous red urukú paint. The phallus of the Umutina men is covered by a little straw cap. In the area back of the spirits hut, which is forbidden to women during the festivities, hang rolled up bundles of buriti palm straw, which the men wind around their bodies. These constitute the skirts of the spirit masqueraders.

69 *The fertility dances of the Carajá and Javahé Indians*

Alongside the water on the great sandbanks of the Araguaya River, stands a row of houses. Farther back is a lone hut, which is the masking house of the Carajá and Javahé Indians. Here live the young fellows, separated from their relatives in the village, until they get married. Then every one of them builds his own hut in the long row near the water. The sacred masks of the tribe are kept in the masking house.

During the whole summer, from early afternoon until late into the evening, masked couples dance. Rhythmically they beat the dance rattle, accompanying it with singing, and with dancing steps they cross the long stretch of sand leading to the houses where groups of women and girls in their ancient traditional garb await them. The females are clothed only in loin aprons made of bast; their bodies are beautifully decorated in black painted geometrical patterns.

Two women or girls approach the masqueraded male dancers with elegant graceful steps, singing, dancing, and beating rattles. They follow in the men's footsteps, halt halfway, stamp in the same place, and at the same time rub their bodies with both hands. Now the masqueraded men turn back, continue until they get close to the masking house, the female dancers still following them. Then the females turn around and, half running, go back to the squatting women close to the huts.

Soon the singing starts, and with beating rattles and short steps a new masked pair comes out of the masking hut in the interior of the sandbank. The couple is still at a distance and their voices are low, but they become louder and louder until they reverberate along the sandbanks. Two girls start out to meet them. The same game is repeated. The masqueraded ones sing ancient verses in language which is not now completely understood. Occasionally new songs are created, which become common property when their rhythmic melodies and words find favor.

The masking house is the domain of the men. No woman would ever dare under any circumstances to try to solve its mystery. If she did she would become the prisoner of the young fellows, and would have to stay there. In earlier times this kind of curiosity was punished by death.

Despite the close and constantly widened contacts with the whites, it is likely that the sacred Aruanã mask dance of the Javahé and Carajá Indians, on the fabulously beautiful Araguaya River, will continue as far as the near future is concerned.

70–71 *Indian children lead a happy, independent life*

Their parents are concerned about them, yet their daily toil keeps them so occupied that they cannot pay continuous attention to the boisterous romping of the young. Nature is ample and enticing and tempts strongly the adventurous spirit of youth, and one day the little ones playing in calm waters ventured too far away from home.

In former times there were thousands of dangerous crocodiles. Today there are still numberless snapping fish. Despite the repeated warning of the mother, the little ones pay scant heed. Then one early afternoon, silent masked Lateni appear on the wide sandbanks, carrying long sticks. The frightened cry of 'Lateni' is heard. All small boys and girls take to flight, run into the airy summer straw huts, and, hiding in the farthest corner, wrap themselves in a blanket and crowd around their mother. The Lateni masks sneak around the house, whistle softly, and peek through the door and the straw walls. Suddenly they stretch out an arm through the straw wall, grab a girl by the hand or by her long hair, but the mother defends her brood against the silent and fearful masks. She struggles with them, until both fall into the calm waters of the beach, to the joy of everyone. However, the high-spirited and always happy Indian young soon forget the half-jocular but half-frightening masks and romping again wander away from the village in the sand, the water, and the forest until the worried mother calls once more on the Lateni masks to help her safeguard her children. So at least has the author understood the appearance of these religious but little known masked apparations from the sacred masking house of the Carajá Indians.

72 *Virgin initiation among the Tucunas*

The tree comes in masquerade from the forest. Strange flute notes come from the forest that surrounds the house of the Tucunas. In the festive house the many guests shake their rattles, sing, and dance. Now the flute's notes are coming nearer!

In the open place in front of the Indian house stands a slim, tall figure. It is completely wrapped in a white garment made of bast with varicolored decorations. A headpiece of light yellow green palm strips sticks out the top. On this are attached small triangles carved from pulp, which look like touched-up leaves. The garment is completed with an appendage below, made of yellow-green palm straw that hangs down like a skirt.

The masqueraded figure stands motionless. It holds a leaf stalk of a papaya tree, and blows long-drawn-out single tones on it. They sound, sweet, sad, and lonely. It is a tree of the forest, which comes to the Tukuna initiation feast.

Actually the tree represents the embodiment of all the evil spirits of the forest, but as a mask it does not seem to possess all these evil characteristics, for like all the other masked figures, it is there to add jollification to the feast and to amuse the guests.

73 *Virgin initiation of the Tucuna Indians*

Monkey and parrot masks come to the initiation feast. Many kinds of masks are worn by guests at the initiation feast: the father of the winds, with a tremendous head, gigantic elephantlike ears, long pointed teeth, and large eyes; butterflies; the spider; the monsters of the deep; parrots (picture left); gigantic serpents, and many others, according to the talent and inspiration of the performers.

But the gayest and most impudent are the monkey masks (see picture in the center and right). The monkeys romp madly around the house. They seize the hut in which the young girl is still held in seclusion, and the relatives and guests jokingly beat off the pantomime attack of the masks. The whistling monkeys, because of their repulsive habits, are disliked. The ringing laughter of the hundreds of guests accompanies the boisterous pranks of the monkey masks of those who imitate the animals they represent.

The masked guests carry wonderfully carved or colorfully painted canes made from balsa wood or sticks (see picture) on which the fruits of the forest are suspended as rattles. At the dance they will be thrust on the wooden floor of the big Tucuna house. The rattle stick takes the place of the gourd rattle, maracá, which is entirely unknown to the Tucuna Indians. The rattle stick is a rough staff, from which the bast has not been removed. It is at least three feet and an inch or so thick.

The above mentioned masks have no religious significance. They are secular. Anyone can touch the wearers and dance with them. Everyone enjoys the usually impudent pranks of the masked people. They symbolize the allegorical spirits which in the past harmed virgins, because relatives and parents did not carry out the ritual of initiation in the proper time and manner.

74 *Behind the sacred masking house of the Javahé and Carajá Indians*

The Javahés and Carajás are familiar with photography and dislike the taking of pictures inside the masking house, because a photograph may acquaint the women and girls, against their will, with its mysteries and they would have to be heavily punished in accordance with tribal tradition.

There are masking houses which are shaped like a hut, with three walls, one in front, and one at each side, but with the back of the house open. Other huts are open with only a screen in front. If the women happen to pass such a hut when on the river, they turn away their heads or cover their faces with both hands.

Behind the straw screen of the masking house are stored the masquerade costumes. The headgear is hung on posts driven into the ground. The long spiral straw skirts are carelessly laid on the floor or tied to a post. In the masking house live the young men, but the grownup and married men also spend some time there when they want to rest from domestic cares or are taking part in the dances.

Here the young men learn craftmanship, and prepare new masks and costumes. They spend the hot time of the day in the shade of the house, and sleep under the open sky at night on a straw mat which is spread on the soft and warm sand.

As long as a young man lives in the masking house, and is a bachelor, he is supported by the villagers. If he marries he must then take care of himself and his family. Young men of this tribe, therefore, often prefer to remain for a long time unmarried.

The masks belong to a young man whom one could call the master of ceremonies. If he dies, the masks must be burned; but masks must be made anew for the religious fertility festivals of the dry season.

75 An Urukú Indian woman removes her son's eyebrows

With the exception of the hair on their heads, the Indians love to remove all growth of hair from their bodies. Indeed some tribes go so far as to shave part of the head to form a tonsure, or shave off the hair up to the middle of the head. They employ as a razor a straight bamboo strip, the husk, which is as sharp as a steel razor.

The Urukús remove eyebrows and other hair in a peculiar manner. The Indian woman holds one end of a thread in her mouth and the other she grips tightly in her right hand. With the fingers of her left hand she closes a knot in the thread which she has looped over a hair in the boy's eyebrow, and this pulls it out.

Mother and son sit on a straw mat in front of the house. The straw mat which stands up straight is used as an outside door. The Carajás and many other tribes simply take some hot ashes between the points of their fingers and hold the hair they want to remove over the ashes; it becomes rough and frizzles and can then be easily torn out.

The Crahós are acquainted with grass seeds and barbed hooks with which a single hair can be caught and pulled out. There are many ways in which unwanted hair growth can be removed. To the Indian the ideal human body is totally hairless, but they value very much the hair on the head.

76–77 Boat-building among the Cashináua

During an expedition in 1951 to the Cashináuas, on the Curanja River near the south of the Purus, the Indians, under the direction of a capable Peruvian noncommissioned officer, fashioned a dugout out of a single mahogany trunk. It was thirty-three feet long and weighed about a ton. The boat had to be carved out with axes and was a masterpiece of craftsmanship. Since it was made deep in the forest, it had to be dragged with great effort by the entire Cashináua tribe to the nearest creek, which was practically dry.

It soon became clear that the water level at this time of the year, even after many days journeying up the river, would be too low. Then the Cashináua employed a new method for the moving of the heavy boat. They chopped off thick pieces of imbauba trunks, which under the soft bark have a very slippery layer and these were laid like rollers in the creek bottom, enabling them to push the heavy boat down the bed of the stream. For twelve days the brave Peruvian noncommissioned officer worked with a handful of Indians and the author to bring our expedition boat to navigable waters (see picture 89).

78 Two Cashináua Indians take a boat ride, on the Curanja River

The Cashináua are not experienced boatbuilders; their craft are small and shapeless. They have apparently tried to imitate the boatbuilding of their neighbors, the Marináuas, who produce splendid long straight dugouts. The Marináuas are masters in manipulating their boats, covering great stretches of water, and overcoming all kinds of obstacles, be they rapids, trunks of trees lying across streams, or other simular impediments.

The stern of the boats of the Marináuas and Cashináuas is wide; one can stand in it during the ride. The favorite implement for moving the boat is a long, strong pole. The man in the stern gives the boat a push with it, so that it moves forward. The Indian in the bow guides the dugout through obstacles in the stream. These duties, however, can be exchanged.

Other tribes make light tree bark canoes which can be used with safety.

79 Cashináua boys watch a dance

Among Indians squatting, is perfectly normal, it is practiced from early childhood. Indians can spend a long time in this position; they relax as we do when we sit down. The Cashináua boys are interested spectators at a dance being performed by adults after a successful fishing expedition. The males among the Cashináua wear their hair short; for haircutting they now use steel scissors. In the past they shaved their heads with a sharp sliver of bamboo.

80 *Makú women in a hammock*

The mutual removal of unwelcome guests in the hair of the head is not an infrequent friendly gesture to be observed among the Indians. If one sees a youth trustfully put his head on the lap of a young girl, one can take for granted that they are sweethearts. The little animals when caught are frequently eaten and it is considered a pleasure to eat those filled with the blood of a loved one. In our picture two Makú women are portrayed who, during this procedure, are comfortably lying in a hammock.

Primitive peoples have no sure means of getting rid of their ancient plague. Modern chemical preparations are frequently received with joy, for its frees them in minutes from the torturing spirits they have never been able to overcome. Out of the helplessness of man against these animals there has developed the virtue of mutal help, which has become a kind of fondling.

81 *Suyá Indians sleep wearing wooden disks*

In the entire world there are only some sixty Suyá Indians. Of this number about eight of them are married men, the remainder are women and youngsters. Only married men wear what we consider grotesque wooden disks in their perforated and enlarged lower lip.

The Suyá sleep in attractive hammocks, which are woven from palm bast threads. The lip disk is not removed even when they go to sleep.

The Suyá man in our picture has lost an eye. A wood splinte hit him when a tree was being cut down. He wears a head-piece made of palm leaf strips. Every Indian can in a few seconds prepare such headgear, to be worn on a fishing expedition, after a successful hunt, or purely as an ordinary adornment. It has no deeper significance than a simple ornament.

82–83 *Crahó Indians traveling*

Families camp together on marches. They rest after hours of wandering through the hot savanna. Just like our own children, Indian youngsters become cranky when they are tired and voice their discomfort by crying. The grandmother and grandfather (picture 83) take care of the youngsters, fondle them, take them on their laps, and the children are soon pacified.

Usually, however Indian children are quite satisfied and good-natured. Older sisters and brothers are willing to take care of them with affection.

84 *The Crahó in the open*

Indians love to sleep in the open. In the Crahó villages, the boys and bachelors fix sleeping quarters for themselves on the village square. A short straw mat, which reaches only to the knee, is spread on the sand. A lively little fire warms up the soles of the feet. From time to time the sleeper awakes and adjusts the log. By dawn the fire has long been dead. If it rains, the boys move into some empty hut, partly to sleep and partly to spend the time talking.

On hunting expeditions in which men alone take part, the sleeping quarters consist of a pair of palm leaves. The dew moistens the naked bodies of the sleepers.

85 *Carajá boy in festive adornment*

Only a few years ago there were in the Carajá and Javahé villages boys, especially the sons of medicine men, who ran around festively adorned all day long. Nowadays if one visits an Indian village on the almost limitless sandbanks of the Araguaya River in central Brazil, one frequently finds festively adorned children, who are dressed up for the purpose of being photographed, for today the Indians demand pay before they permit their pictures to be taken.

Our picture of a Carajá boy was taken about fifteen years ago. Today he is a married man. It portrays a boy who had a privileged position in Indian society, and could be seen only when he was wearing festive ornaments. In the perforated lip, the boy is wearing a thin bone, with a thick end, which is fastened between the lower jaw and the lip so that it cannot fall out.

In his perforated earlobes are flower decorations made of colorful ara feathers. From the mother-of-pearl disk in the center protrudes the tooth of a water hog. This is the most precious ornament of the tribe, for teeth of a young water hog of the exactly prescribed size are difficult to come by.

The feathers are fastened to a stick of wood that is inserted in the hole in the earlobe.

The upper arms to just below the elbow are wrapped in cotton cord dyed black, the ends of which drag on the ground.

On the forearms the Carajá boy wears knitted cotton wrist bands, which have oily blood-red urukú paint rubbed on them. The face and body of the child are painted bright red. The hair is greased. The glass beads have been obtained in trade from the whites, or in payment for permission to be photographed.

86 Virgin initiation among the Tucunas: the weaving of a sitting mat from palm strips

At the close of the festivities of virgin initiation among the Tucunas, a straw mat is woven, on which the girl must sit when her hair is being torn out by the women.

Despite the European clothing, which has taken the place of bast, the tribal traditions have for the most part survived. A girl who does not submit to the ritual of virgin initiation is hardly considered in the tribe as a fullcledged woman.

87 A Cashináua woman weaves a sitting mat from a young palm leaf with a leaf border

For the purpose of weaving sitting mats and baskets, the Indians use mostly unopened young palm leaves, which are just beginning to shoot forth from the top of the tree. The straw of such shoots is soft and easy to use. When it dries it becomes somewhat hard and unpliable. If they want a stiffer mat they weight it with the spine of the palm leaf, from which the leaf feathers hang down.

88 Pottery among the Carajá and Javahé Indians

Pots are broken every day, and every day an Indian woman is busy with the task of replacing them. Every Indian woman knows how to fashion earthenware pottery.

The clay is to be found not far away from Carajá and Javahé villages. Somewhere there is a steep bank where it can be obtained. The Indians form the clay into small hand-sized balls, and dry them in the hot sun. On the banks of the rivers and lakes river sponges hang on brushwood. They are black and prickly and are round as a ball. They contain innumerable silica crystals which are necessary for the mixing of the clay. Without these crystals the clay vessels would burst in the process of firing.

The Indian woman carries these sponges to the open fire and burns them, then she mixes the ashes in equal part with the crushed clay. She adds water, and first forms the bottom, then the sides, and in the process the pot assumes the shape typical of an Indian vessel. Now she takes a spoon – in the past she used a mussel shell – and starts to scrape. The sides of the pot become smooth, the edges soft and even. Soon the pot is put to dry in the hot sun.

The next day the Indian woman puts it on three small cones made from burned clay and piles wood under, around and across it. The flames spring high and cover the pot, the form glows, and when the flame is extinguished, she removes the pot, which is now so hard it clinks when it is tapped.

All kinds of clay vessels are made every day: cooking pots, bowls, and plates, water vessels and urns. Some are colorfully painted with very beautiful patterns decorating the sides and the inside. Only the kitchenware is one color.

89 The conveyance of the dugout of the expedition through the shallow water of the Cetico Brook in the source region of the Purus

Yard after yard is covered. The boat is heavy and the water is shallow. It will take days before it is deep enough so that the boat can float freely. The upper courses of the rivers dry up fast in the summer. During the rainy season, the upper courses become wild raging, streams. (See also pictures 76–77).

90 The big hut of the Cashináua Indians on the Upper Curanja River

This rectangular straw house stands in the midst of a banana grove. It does not appear as long as it really is. It must be at least eighty-three feet in length. The roof wings nearly reach the ground. It is gloomy in these big Cashináua houses. The floor is stamped hard and is cleanly swept. Some ten to twenty families live there together, and there are as many hearths. Each family can recognize its particular place in the hut by its hearth. The cotton hammocks are hung on the crossbeams of the house. There is a chief for every house. This one is called Tuchaua.

91 *Joint family house of the Urukú Indians*

The Urukús live in the dense primeval forests of the Gy-Paraná River. Joint families inhabit the same hut. Straw is tied on the beams to keep the rain out. The walls touch the ground and it is very dark inside. Only in the narrow circle of the hearth which every family has can one recognize those who are working there. The smoke goes out through the straw roof and the scraps from the preparation of food are simply thrown out through a hole in the wall.

Many hammocks are fastened all around. They are much shorter than the bodies of those who lie in them, either to rest or to sleep.

92 *The Cashináua women weave highly artistic hammocks*

Their hammocks woven from cotton are known and are in demand in the entire region of the Upper Purus. The Marináua, a neighboring tribe of the Cashináuas, spend many days traveling along the entire Curanja River in order to obtain new hammocks from the Cashináua. The fact that they are not always treated fairly is because the Marináua possess firearms and the poor Cashináua only bows and arrows. Just the same, the Marináua pay for their goods. An old steel ax or a knife is exchanged for a hammock which took nearly a month to make.

The men sow the cotton seed in their fields and the women pick the ripe bolls, seed them, twist the threads and roll them into immense balls. A part of the thread is dyed with color extract made from roots and tree bark: black, brown, light blue, or yellow. The loom consists of two round poles. The warp is bound by cord, which fastens it to the poles. One end of the loom hangs on a post, the other is fastened like a sling around the Indian woman's body.

She starts the weaving at each end, and to facilitate her work, poles are passed through the long lower weft. As the two woven parts meet each other, the last threads must be pulled through with a thin bone needle and great care must be taken that no unevenness occurs.

The same geometrical pattern of this beautiful hammock is to be found on other woven work, on pottery and weapons, and the painting of the body of the Cashináua. Nothing is definitely known regarding its meaning or origin.

93 *A piece cut from a decorated masquerade garment of the Tucuna*

The garments of the Tucuna masquerade are made of beaten bast. Bast is the layer of fiber between bark and the trunk of certain trees. There is brown as well as white bast fiber. It is loosened from the trunk by the knocking it with a cudgel. The masquerade garments of the Tucuna are colorfully decorated. The geometric and traced plant patterns show the influence of their civilized neighbors, the Peruvians and Brazilians. This and other drawings, which appear in colored pictures which follow in this book, are of genuine Indian origin. The colors are pure natural products. They fade out quickly and they are supposed to remain pretty and colorful only during the few days of the virgin initiation. The yellow is saffron that the Tucunas plant. The red is the pulp of the fruit of the urukú shrub, which is cultivated by all Indians. The green is the chlorophyl of the mashed pupunha palm leaf. The blue is obtained from the fruit of a native suffrutescent plant which they call naiku. The color at first is deep blue-black, which changes quickly to blue, red-blue, bright blue, and then completely fades out!

94 *A burial urn from the Marajó Island in the estuary delta of the Amazon River*

Before the discovery of Brazil various Indian tribes alternately inhabited the Marajó Island. One of those tribes produced highly artistic ceramics. Today no Indians live on the Marajó, but remains are found in the so-called 'tesos,' artificial mounds which were used for dwelling and burial places. These provided protection for the inhabitants against the annual floods that lasted for several months. Little is known of the tribe that produced the wonderful ceramics, but one can state with assurance that they were an agricultural people, that they lived in communities, and that at first their dead were buried in ordinary graves and several years later the bones were placed in artistic urns.

The urn in our picture is about thirty-two inches high. It was found inside a large plain urn without any kind of artistic decoration. The color of the urn in our picture is iron red, creamy white, and in some places bright red. Because of the annual floods, other original colors may have been washed away. Urns of wonderful color combinations and highly artistic workmanship have been found on the Marajó Island. Some of them are now in the great museums of the world, especially at Belem do Pará, Rio de Janeiro, Philadelphia, and Oslo.

95–96 *Bleeding*

From time to time almost all Indians have to be bled. A triangular piece of bottle gourd with inserted fish teeth is the necessary surgical instrument. The medicine man or some other Indian applies it and pulls it energetically. The plentifully spurting blood is wiped away with a piece of palm leaf. Then the wound is washed out in the river. Finally, the Indian rubs green pepper pods and leaves between the palms of his hands, then massages the long wound.

Bleeding is the concern of men, and women are seldom permitted to perform this operation. The Carajá and Javahé have long scars on their bodies, and they declare that after a strong bleeding they feel very much better.

97 *A Cashináua Indian cures his infected hand*

The hand with the infected and swollen finger hurts. Indians do not have any means of stopping pain. In order to provide the necessary rest for the hand, the sick Indian has fastened a bast loop on the roof beam. He has inserted his infected hand in it. Now perhaps he may be able to sleep if the pain permits it. The medicine man may order repeated baths with an infusion of healing herbs. Rest and time are here the most trustworthy means of healing. Loud weeping of the relatives announce to the entire village that a tribesman has fallen sick.

98 *The Crahó medicine man or shaman treats a sick child*

The child has a headache, it is pale. The parents are worried. The father has attempted with the best means at his disposal to help. Finally it is decided to call the medicine man. He taps the child and diagnoses at once that this is no mortally dangerous sickness and that it may be a case of slight constipation. The medicine man massages the body and the head of the child and finally blows the pain out of the hair on the crown of the head. The medicine man receives for his treatment a pot of food and perhaps a piece of game.

99–100 *To be a medicine man or shaman among the Crahós is a dangerous occupation*

Among the Crahó Indians there are two kinds of medicine men, the vaiaká, the good ones, and kói, the evil ones. The good shamans, or medicine men, occupy themselves only with healing, either by use of herbs or magical treatment. The kói have a reputation of secretly burying evil magic to bring misfortune to their fellowmen or to destroy them entirely.

When he begins his occupation, every medicine man is a vaiaká or a good magician. Only later may he acquire a dangerous reputation of occupying himself with evil magic. Frequently his behavior contributes to this reputation. He may throw out threats against his fellowmen that he will punish them with evil magic if they are not docile. Should the community come to believe that the deaths which have occurred are due to the evil medicine man, a secret council may condemn him to death. It is understandable that when it appears to be absolutely necessary to the survival of the tribe that he be eliminated, his execution will be authorized. Medicine men usually have much more power in the tribe than the chief, possibly because of the fear which the Indians have of their supposed knowledge and association with the supernatural. Among the Crahós medicine men, or shamans, are very much liked, but since they are considered social outsiders they cannot compete in power with the village chiefs. The medicine man in pictures 99 and 100 is removing evil substances which have caused illness in a young woman. By massage he has concentrated the foreign magic in one spot, sucked it out, and spat it on the ground.

Indian medicine men have ample knowledge in the matter of employing healing plants of their native regions. Our scientific medicine owes them a great deal for many medicinal herbs.

101 *A young Cashináua Indian takes leave of his wife who has just died*

102 *The Carajás bury the bones of their dead in urns*

Some years after the first burial, they exhume the bones of the departed and bury them a second time in earthenware urns, which they deposit on the flat ground. They are sealed up with a flat lid. Hundreds of urns are deposited in the cemetery on a high bank in the forest near the river, where the winds blow over them. Fallen branches break the covers and even some of the urns. From time to time they are visited by relatives, mostly women, who place small vessels with food and dainties near the urns. In some cemeteries, which may be centuries old, the urns are piled up inside large earth mounds. Other Indian tribes pulverize the bones of their dead and mix them with beverages. The blood relatives partake of them during the rituals of the dead. The idea of eternal life is present in this sacred rite. The departed one is thought to live again in the body of the living kin, becomes one with him, and thus is saved from death, a fate every living creature fears.

103 *Watching over the sickbed*

In former times the Indians were not subject to many ailments. The tribes lived widely apart and there were not many contagious maladies. Today epidemics rage through the forests carried in by rubber gatherers and by Indians who have visited whites: these include measles, whooping cough, influenza, scarlet fever, smallpox, venerial diseases, and tuberculosis. Most of these diseases are fatal to the Indians. They have exterminated hundreds of tribes whose names are no longer known. They are still running their destructive course despite precautions being taken by the appropriate authorities. Human life is lost every day, which under normal conditions would have been saved. In the isolation of the forest entire tribes are still subject to extermination because there are no adequate means to organize help for them. Where are the rescuers of these lonely, helpless, lovable, and worthty primitive human beings?

104 *Laments for the dead*

Loud lamentation is heard in the quietness of the Crahó village which lies in the hot glare of the noon sun on the broad savanna. It comes from a house in which for a long time a boy has been sick. Relatives and friends gather hastily. The lamentation becomes louder, interrupted by chanting and the poetic words of the mourners who glorify the departed. Rhythmically the lamentation, chanting, and glorification are repeated. The nude body of the dead boy lies on his straw mat. He is washed by his parents and relatives and then painted with bright red urukú paint. It is the last festive painting. Red is the color of life.

Soon the pallbearers will come. The corpse will be wrapped in a mat, tied lengthwise to a pole, and then carried to a nearby cemetery.

A rectangular grave, about forty inches deep, is dug and then lined with wood and covered with branches; then earth is put on top of it. This is to prevent animals from digging the body out. In the house of mourning, the relatives and friends weep and chant, glorifying the departed boy. Outside in the village, daily life with all its toil and care resumes its course.

105 *A Crahó Indian is being festively painted by his wife*

Indians paint their bodies not only for festivities, but also for everyday adornment. The most used colors are red and black. Yellow and white are employed less often. Red and black are made from plant juices; yellow and white are colors derived from clay. A group of festively decorated Indians is an unforgettably splendid sight.

In this picture, Capró greases her husband Cratchet with rubberlike juice. As soon as it dries, she rubs in the vertical lines with charcoal. The decoration lasts several days, then it becomes unsightly and slowly fades. The places between the stripes are colored with oily red urukú paint. Depending on whether a Crahó tribesman belongs to the half tracing its origin to the moon, or that which is descended from the sun, the stripes painted on the body are either vertical or horizontal. Other relationships in the social life of the tribe are given expression through the manner in which the body is painted. Fluid rubber is gathered by the women from cutting tops of palm shoots, such as Capró is holding in her hand.

106–107 *Cashináua man and woman with artfully decorated faces*

Artistic body painting is the everyday adornment of the Cashináuas. The women are the painters. With a flexible stick, which has a small roll of cotton wrapped around one end, they draw freehand the geometrical patterns on the faces of their husbands. The same patterns are repeated in weaving, spinning, pottery, little stools, mortars, and weapons. Only the bodies of men are adorned with wide dark surfaces that emphasize the muscular strength of the male sex. Women's bodies are decorated with more delicate lines and rows of dots.

Every few days the Cashináua spend a good deal of time carefully decorating their bodies and faces.

On festive occasions the men wear splendid feather headpieces obtained from the japu birds whose nests hang like long black stockings from the treetops. In their perforated nostrils the Cashináua men wear the long tail feathers of the red ara. The women have the septum of their noses perforated and, as an ornament, some of them carry a half moon cut from mother-of-pearl taken from the shell of a river mussel. The Cashináua are peaceful farmers.

108–115 *Hand-carved necklace of the Tucunas made of hard palm nuts*

An elderly deaf-and-dumb Tucuna woman is the greatest artistic craftswoman of her tribe. All Tucuna women and girls wear pretty necklaces, which they have made for themselves from the hard tucum palm nuts, but not one of them has the artistic ability of this old Indian craftswoman.

Like many thousand Tucunas she lives in one of the houses erected on piles way back along one of the small creeks that runs into the Upper Amazon. With a knife stump, because until recently she did not have a better tool to work with, all day long with wearying labor she incorporates her ideas in palm nuts. She gives artistic expression to the faces she sees in her dreams, as well as the legends of the tribes and the happenings of her daily life. The finished figures are smoothed out with sand and polished with a soft sliver of wood, until they are black and shiny.

Every Tucuna girl and woman wears these carved wooden necklaces. Everyone carves small birds, reptiles, fish, and insects from the hard tucum nuts of their forests. It is the typical ornament of the tribe. But none reaches the high artistic perfection of the necklace shown in our picture.

116 *Painting on bast material by Tucuna Indians (like 93-117-118)*

Two Brazilians or Peruvians are portrayed wearing hats, clothing, and shoes and smoking cigarettes. In the decorations they paint on the bast material of the masquerade garments for the virgin initiation, they give an important place to things they have seen among their civilized neighbors. One often sees river steamers, airplanes, soldiers, churches, and other objects, which the Tucunas have seen on their visits to the cities of the Upper Amazonas, such as São Paulo de Olivença, Benjamin Constant, and Tabatinga in Brazil,

Leticia in Colombia, and Iquitos in Peru. There may even be some Indians among the Tucunas who have served as members of the crew of one of the great steamers that ply the Amazon, and may actually have seen the capital city, Manaus, or have been to Belém do Pará, a city with a population of half a million people on the estuary of the Amazon.

117 *A jaguar drawing on bast material; Tucuna Indians*

A jaguar is not only a good model for artistic endeavor, but it has a special meaning in the life of the Indians. In the forest it is the most powerful and most feared beast of prey, and the hunter who succeeds in killing one wins great renown. In the old tales told around the hearth, and in tribal traditions, it plays a very important role.

Knowing the behavior of the animal, one would suppose that the jaguar would be portrayed as an especially crafty and superior beast. But this is not the case. Jaguars and turtles appear in many Indian myths and legends as playing against each other. The turtle personifies the sly creature who never fails to put it over on the doltish and stupid jaguar. The monkey also plays one trick after another on the jaguar who attempts to catch him. In a tale of Caingang of southern Brazil, it is related how the monkey rode on the back of the jaguar to an animal feast and then upon arrival dismissed him, and the jaguar never succeeded in participating in the festivities, though the monkey promised him that he would. To this day, in revenge, the jaguar tries to entrap the turtle, the monkey, and other animals that appear in these tales. In other myths the spots of the jaguar are symbolized as a constellation.

118 *Painting on bast material of the Tucunas*

The sketched bird is a so-called mutum, which resembles the European woodcock. It is valued as game by both the Indians and the whites. It reaches the size of a fat domestic chicken. The colors of the picture are the fancy free creation of the Indian painter. In reality the bird is black with dark, metallic, shiny wing and neck feathers. It has a big red knobby beak and red legs. A smaller species has a yellow beak and yellow legs. The Umutinas prefer not to kill the mutum. They like to bring up the young of this early maturing bird themselves.

Upon the death of an Umutina one of the three human

souls may be transferred to the captured bird, and henceforth he is known as the soul-carrying bird, a relative of the Indians, and is loved and taken care of. The soul-carrying birds are never given away or killed.

The tribal mark of the Umutinas is a feather ornament fastened with clay on the upper arm and is made of the breast feathers of the mutum.

119–126 *Toys made from burnt clay*

All human beings give toys to their children. The Carajá women of the Araguaya River make clay dolls for their youngsters. In former times they were preponderately simple human shapes – a body without arms, wide hips, and spindly legs and feet. The children play with them by sticking them in the soft, white, omnipresent sand on the great sandbanks where the Carajás live in the summer. But the few whites who occasionally visited the domain of the Carajás found these gaily painted clay figurines beautiful and exotic, and soon they began to be traded. The Indian women then proceeded to fire these breakable figurines, in order to make them more durable. They also began to create new shapes.

In the course of some decades, they have gone through various phases of artistic creation. They have made by turns figurines which were reflections of their tribal myths, likenesses from their dreams, and embodiment of their ideas. There were all kinds of expressions of human pain and joy. But besides that, they have always used clay to make for the children and curious whites representations of the animal world of their native region. These figurines are primitive, some of them are lumpy, but all have the charactistics appropriate to the animal species being portrayed, despite their imperfections of form and decoration.

119 *Jaguar*

120 *Armadillo*

121 *Jaguar made of wax with straw ornaments*

122 *Toad*

123 *Heron*

124 *Bittern*

125 *Gray heron*

126 *Umutina boy about eight years old*

The long hair is tied in a knot in the back (not visible here). In his perforated earlobes are inserted rings made of carved palm nuts, from which hang colored feather ornaments. On the upper arm is placed the tribal mark of the Umutinas, a feather ornament. With the left hand he grasps a bow and arrow, which are made in proportion to his size. Ikodo's eyes betray the pride of his race, and the waggish face expresses the superiority of feeling, characteristic of the man of the primeval forest, over against the whites, who are dependent upon him in his native heath. It seems benevolently contemptuous to say: We have our own world!

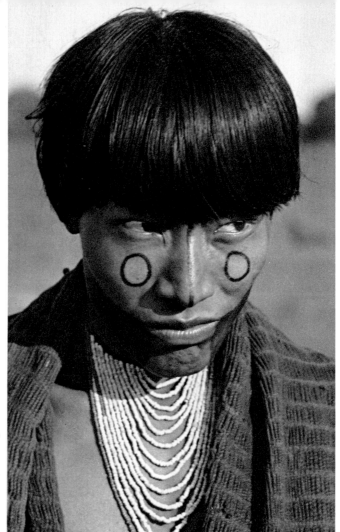

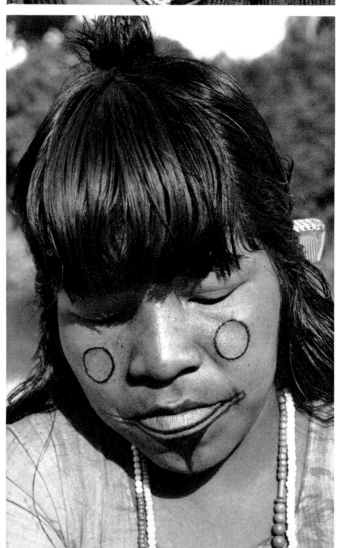

25

27

26

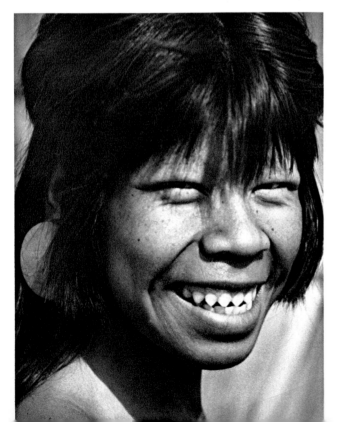

41

47

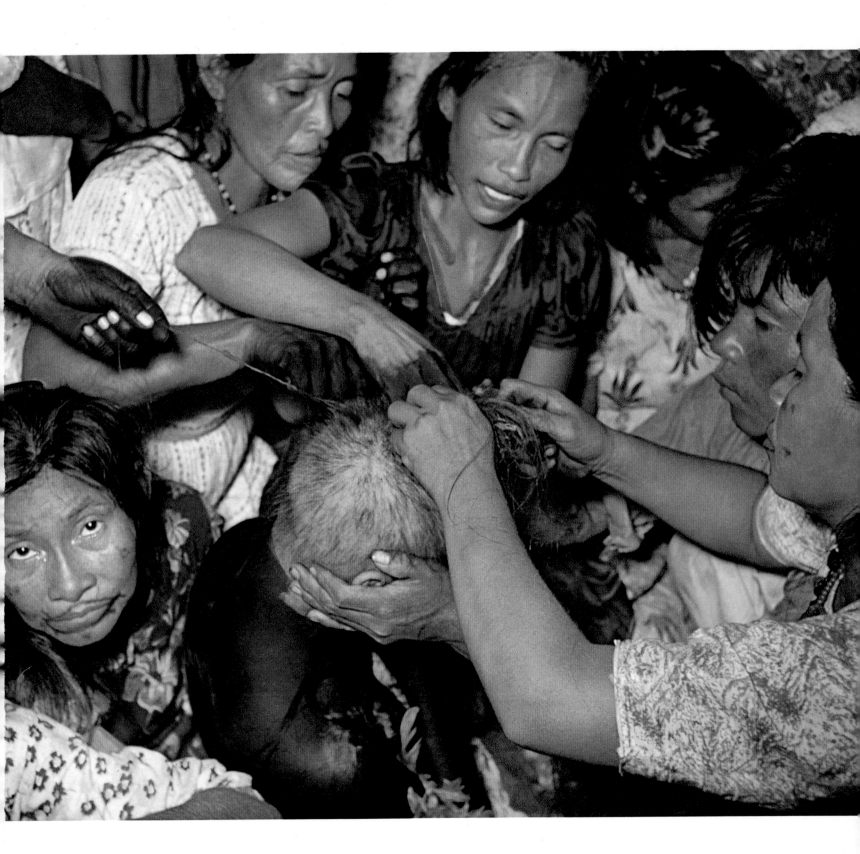

70

71

79

80

81

82

83

84

91

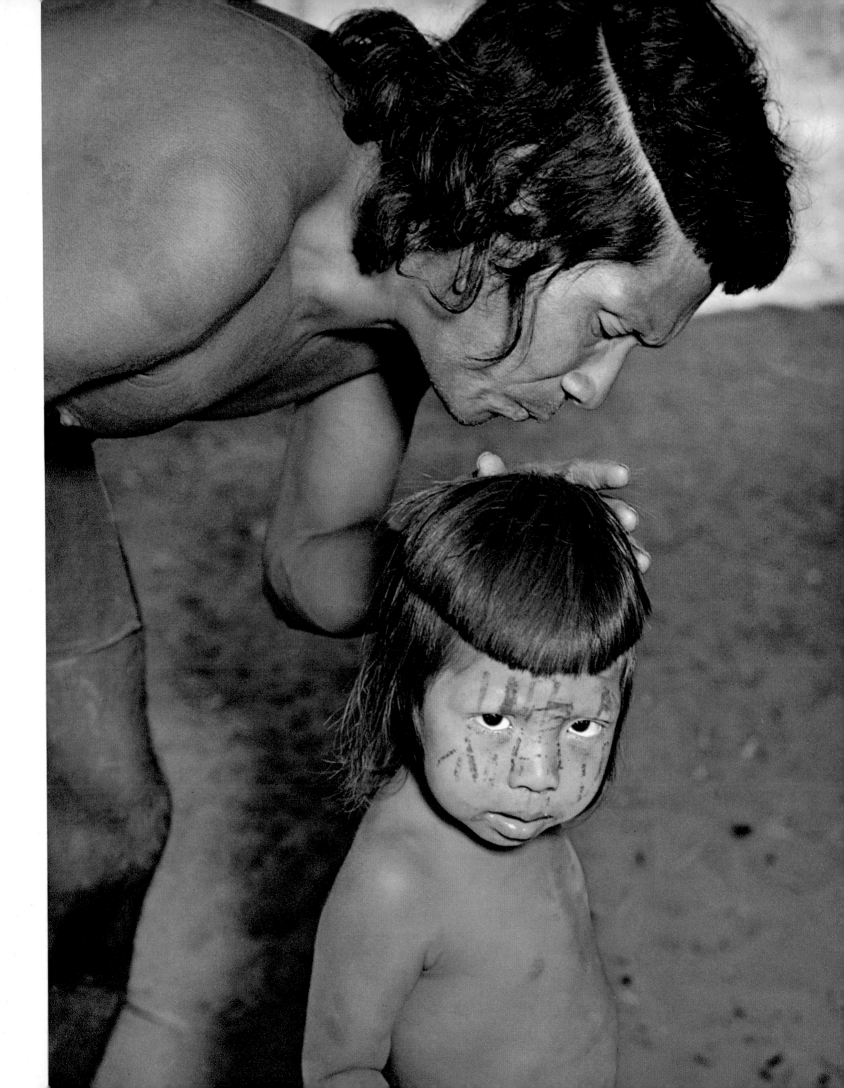

109

110

111

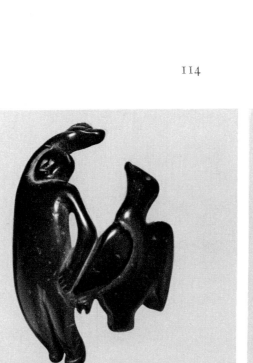

113

112

114

115

119   120

121   122

123   124   125